William E. Phipps has taught at several colleges and universities, and is currently Chair of the Department of Religion and Philosophy at Davis and Elkins College. Dr. Phipps has degrees from several colleges and universities around the world including Davidson College (B.S.); the University of Hawaii (M.A.); St. Andrews University, Scotland (Ph.D.). A Presbyterian minister, he has had numerous works published including articles in *The New York Times*, *Theology Today*, *The Christian Century,* and *New Testament Studies*.

PAUL
AGAINST
SUPERNATURALISM

PAUL
AGAINST
SUPERNATURALISM

The Growth of the Miraculous
in Christianity

by
William E. Phipps

Philosophical Library
New York

Library of Congress Cataloging-in-Publication Data

Phipps, William E., 1930-
  Paul against supernaturalism.

  Bibliography: p.
  Includes Index.
  1. Miracles—History of doctrines—Early church,
ca. 30-600.   2. Virgin birth.   3. Jesus Christ—
Resurrection.   4. Jesus Christ—History of doctrines—
Early church, ca. 30-600.   Bible. N.T. Epistles
of Paul—Criticism, interpretation, etc. I. Title.
BS2545.M5P48   1986   231.7'3'0915   85-19228
ISBN 0-8022-2501-2

CONTENTS

5

PREFACE

Across the centuries many Christians have rejected the searching mind associated with the ancient Greek philosophers. According to Celsus, a second century pagan, Christians say: "Do not ask questions, only believe. Faith will save you. Wisdom is an evil thing and foolishness good." Friedrich Nietzsche has reiterated this notion in the modern era: "Every straightforward, honest, scientific road to knowledge has to be repudiated by the church as a forbidden road.... 'Faith' means not wanting to know what is true." *Time* essayist Roger Rosenblatt, in the wake of recent global bigotry by religious fanatics, contends that reason and religion have always been in unresolvable conflict. He declares: "Faith is belief without reason. Fundamentally, religions oppose rational processes." Rosenblatt presumes that the apostle Paul would agree.

This work of historical theology and biblical interpretation is written with the hope that it will help to break down the compartmentalization that has continually separated Christian convictions from rational and scientific understandings. I reject the frequent viewpoint of both believers and non-believers that anti-intellectualism is intrinsic to Christianity. Many educated people now accept the logical theories of mathematics and the empirical methods of science as a primary way to obtain truth. However, some educated people with a Christian orientation cannot integrate truths about nature with the creeds of their religion. They presume that the prime movers of Christian theology held that religious truth should be piously adored but not rigorously related to scientific findings. Against this I shall argue that Paul, along with some other contributors to the New Testament, presupposed that faith may go beyond, but not against, reason in arriving at truth. Hence, the church's perennial appeal to alleged supernaturalism falsifies the original thrust of Christianity. ·

This book is dedicated to the memory of my father-in-law, Fenton Hendy Swezey. A Presbyterian minister's son, he struggled to emancipate himself from the irrational doctrines that have made Christianity untenable for those with scientific training. I am grateful to him for encouraging me to publish my attempts to grapple with our common concern. My wife, Martha Ann, along with his other children, Catherine and Charles, are now educators. They carry on his passion to reconcile the scientific, literary, and ethical dimensions of human existence with rational religion.

William E. Phipps

Davis and Elkins College
Elkins, West Virginia

INTRODUCTION

The term "supernatural" has been used to designate anything from a haunted house to the hallowed Trinity. It can
refer to what is reportedly unnatural in contrast to what is
scientifically verifiable, or to the spiritual realm in contrast to
the material. In this study "supernatural" is used to describe
alleged happenings that cannot be explained by the ordinary
operations of nature, whether physical or psychical. Hence, a
divine causation is posited to explain those events. In monotheism, a supernaturalist is one who believes that acts of God
interrupt the regular scientific order. William Jennings Bryan
was a famous American supernaturalist. At the Scopes trial he
testified that he not only accepted that a whale swallowed
Jonah but that he would have no difficulty believing that

Johah swallowed a whale, if the Bible affirmed that God had wanted it to happen. Bryan would probably have been comfortable in defining his viewpoint on religion with this dictionary definition of "supernaturalism": "The theological doctrine that the divine is fundamentally different from the temporal order and cannot be approached through its categories.... In this view, faith, revelation, and the authority of Scripture take the place of reason."[1]

Another meaning of "supernatural" is quite separable from the way in which the term is used in this study. It can be used broadly to refer to anything that proceeds from God. In that sense there is in the Judeo-Christian religion a doctrine of supernatural revelation. Creating, sustaining, and liberating are accomplished in the world by the thought and will of God, the ultimate reality. Thus, "supernatural" can refer to a nonpantheistic theology in which God is independent of material nature. The religion of the apostle Paul is "supernatural" in that God is represented as transcendent over nature as well as immanent within it. The logic of the Biblical doctrine of creation is that God minus the universe is still God. Paul Tillich was a supernaturalist, if the term is defined broadly in this way, but he called himself an "antisupernaturalist" with regard to the doctrine that God displays power in the world by violating the natural order.

This study focuses on the spiraling growth of supernaturalism in the early centuries of Christianity. Charismatic figures of biblical history were remembered not so much by what they actually said and did in their lifetimes as by the expanded records of their less inspired hagiographers. After these bigger-than-life caricatures, drawn by adoring disciples, got into common circulation, the humanity of particular historical characters became devalued. Inflation is a problem for interpreters of religious literature as well as for those whose concern is the marketplace. Just as coins of base metal drive out of circulation coins of quality substance, so the authentic earliest record of a religious figure is not as likely to be found in general currency as the tawdry tales with which it has been alloyed.

Compare, for example, Francis Xavier, as he and his contemporaries told of his life, with the Xavier as reconstructed by his later biographers. Neither the letters by that Jesuit missionary nor documents by his sixteenth century contemporaries associate him with supernatural acts. However, four decades after Xavier's death, the early missionary to Eastern Asia is portrayed as stilling a tempest and raising the dead in the biography published by Father Tursellinus. Six decades after his death, Cardinal Monte described ten miracles worked by Xavier, including raising various dead persons, levitation, causing an earthquake, and destroying a town by calling fire down from heaven. Pope Gregory XV was so impressed by the wonders accredited to Xavier that he had him canonized.[2]

Several thousand years before Xavier, the story of Moses in Egypt provides another illustration of the inflation that accompanied heroes. Jumbled together in the book of Exodus are several accounts of the life and times of Moses that were recorded in different centuries, after having been circulated orally for many generations. The literary structure of Exodus resembles a mound left by an ancient town—the different levels that have accumulated tell an archaeologist of the various peoples who lived there at different times. Likewise, textual scholars have painstakenly probed the documents embedded in Exodus and the rest of the Pentateuch to ascertain the chronological development. However, lacking any contemporary Egyptian record about Moses and the Israelites, separating the earliest tradition from the later strata is much more difficult than in the case of Xavier. Moreover, the bloating of a holy man's biography occurs soon after his death, so it is hard to compare the relative exaggeration of records centuries after the time of happening. Even so, some scholars agree that the traditions which were recorded several centuries after the time of Moses have less emphasis on the miraculous than

those supplements made by the priestly editors of the Pentateuch who lived about seven centuries after Moses.[3]

The first two chapters of Exodus, for example, which mainly
record earlier traditions about Moses, contain no reference to
unnatural happenings. There the Israelite slave resistance is
portrayed as instigated by women who are armed with compassion and intelligence. Two midwives deceive their Egyptian
masters in order to save the threatened lives of Hebrew infants.
Baby Moses is protected by his resourceful mother and sister,
and then by Pharaoh's daughter. In the older tradition Moses
does not perform miracles against the Egyptians but does
announce plagues,[4] some of which may be related to natural
scourges that were troublesome in the Nile valley. The latest
writers were Jerusalem priests who had a "tendency to make
the calamity more severe,"[5] so they decorated already inflated
tradition in order to achieve this. Moses becomes more a
supernatural wonder-worker than a believable human.

An extrabiblical romantic legend about Moses, circulated
before the Christian era, heightens Moses' status even more.
Without biblical basis, Greek writer Artapanus depicts Moses
escaping from prison when "the doors of the prison opened of
their own accord." Some of the magical power associated with
Aaron in the Exodus text is transferred to his brother. Moses is
the one who turns a rod into a snake when performing before
Pharaoh. Using his magical rod, Moses strikes the waters of
Egypt and turns them to blood. Moses' rod is also instrumental
in bringing the plagues of frogs and insects.[6]

Between Moses and Xavier in the historical record belongs
the charismatic founder of Christianity. The story of Jesus' life
and of the beginning of the church have been subject to infla-
tionary tendencies similar to those that transformed the life
story of his illustrious predecessors and followers. Regarding
this, New Testament specialist C. Milo Connick has written:
"Miracle stories clustered like grapes about the stem of historical personages. Their aim was to inflate the personal status of

the hero. It was even considered legitimate to manufacture miraculous tales for this purpose."[7] What has happened to central figures in the Judeo-Christian tradition is commonplace in all religions. Magnification through the process of transmission has, for example, resulted in fantastic stories of Mohammed's overnight ride to heaven on his horse and of jewel-laden trees sprouting to herald the Buddha.

In pursuit of the most authentic information about Christian beginnings, it is necessary to disentangle the relevant strands of tradition. Because of the scarcity of ancient sources it is difficult to write as precisely about the growth of legendary material concerning Jesus as it was for Xavier. Nonetheless, more source material exists pertaining to Jesus than to Moses. Throughout this study, as in some of my previous works,[8] I will be anchored in Paul's understandings, which are contained in the oldest surviving Christian documents.

1

THE THIRST FOR UNNATURAL HAPPENINGS

The earliest extant Christian writings contain no accounts of supernaturalism. Paul's letters, which were written a decade or so before the earliest Gospel, do not suggest that God interferes with the natural order. The apostle did occasionally refer to miracles, but he did so from a perspective that is now called Augustinian or Tillichian.

Augustine and Tillich

In interpreting Paul's doctrine, Augustine of Hippo rejects the concept of unnatural happenings. In Romans 11:24 the

15

apostle uses an analogy from horticulture to express his amazement over the way religious history runs counter to expectations. He pictures a wild olive shoot that was grafted "contrary to nature" on a limb of a cultivated olive tree. Augustine comments that " 'contrary to nature' is here used in the sense of contrary to human experience of the course of nature." "God, the Author and Creator of all natures," Augustine reasons, "does nothing contrary to nature; for whatever is done by him who appoints all natural order and measure and proportion must be natural in every case." Consequently, what we call miracles are subjective judgments provoked by our ignorance of the divine order. Augustine explains:

> We give the name nature to the usual common course of nature, and whatever God does contrary to this we call a prodigy or a miracle. But against the supreme law of nature, which is beyond the knowledge both of the ungodly and the weak believers, God never acts, any more than he acts against himself. In regard to spiritual and rational beings, to which class the human soul belongs, the more they partake of this unchangeable law and light, the more clearly they see what is possible and what impossible; and again, the greater their distance from it, the less their perception of the future, and the more frequent their surprise at strange occurrences.[1]

Augustine acknowledges that it was from reading about astronomy that he came to realize the constancy of nature.[2] He observed that "the ignorant multitude" believe Romulus, by divine power, caused solar eclipses because they do not know eclipses are "brought about by the fixed regularity of the sun's course."[3]

However, Augustine's awareness of physical regularities is not closely akin to the modern outlook, for he accepts as natural what current scientists deem contrary to nature. Indeed, his credulity is not atypical of the medieval Christian. Extraordinary happenings, from transforming water into wine to reviving the dead, are considered no more wonderful than the ordinary course of God's creation, even though constant recurrence has dulled our amazement. In reference to Jesus' power to resuscitate corpses, Augustine writes: "A dead man has risen again—people marvel; many are born daily—none marvel. Actually it is a greater wonder for one to be created who did not exist before than for one who was created to come to life again."[4] Since Augustine was frequently insensitive to what Aristotelians called the order of nature, he had no need for a theology positing a divine intervention into its regularities.

Paul Tillich, with a modern philosopher's outlook on natural phenomena, restates the theoretical position of Augustine in his monumental *Systematic Theology*: "Miracles cannot be interpreted in terms of a supranatural interference in natural processes.... A genuine miracle is first of all an event which is astonishing, unusual, shaking, without contradicting the rational structure of reality."[5] In a later discussion Tillich claims his "antisupernaturalistic attitude" is in line with the New Testament.[6] To define a miracle—as C. S. Lewis[7] and others do—as "an interference with nature by supernatural power" is, for Tillich, "distorted because it means that God has to destroy his creation in order to produce his salvation.... God is then split in himself." Tillich continues: "Miracles operate in terms of ordinary causality. To think of them as involving an objective breaking of the structure of reality, or suspending the laws of nature, is superstition."[8] Tillich defines miracle as "the ecstatic, symbolically powerful natural phenomenon," and states that Paul's religion "has all the characteristics of genuine revelation, the ecstatic, the miraculous, the inspirational."[9]

Tillich's usage of the word "miracle" is in accord with its Latin root *miraculum*, meaning an astonishment, and with a main viewpoint of the Bible. Jerome, in his Vulgate, employs *miraculum* to translate biblical terms that designate a marvel.[10] Those terms do not usually carry an overtone of the supernatural but signify God's wonderful acts in nature or splendid deeds of love and justice.[11] R. F. Johnson comments: "In the biblical sense, a miracle is an unusual, marvelous event which testifies to God's active presence in the world. This does not mean, however, that the miracle is a disruption of the natural order."[12] Thus, in the earliest Christian usage, a miracle meant simply an "Oh-my-God!" exclamation on the part of the reverent beholder. The viewpoint that Tillich shares with some early Christians is used here in a chronological exploration of New Testament literature.

Paul's Letters

In English translations of the Greek New Testament, "miracles" is most often used to translate the term *dynameis*, which broadly means "dynamic expressions." Paul uses *dynameis* in several letters (dating from about A.D. 50 to 63) to refer in a general way to marvelous manifestations of God's Spirit in the Gentile communities in which he worked.[13] *Semeia* and *terata*, meaning "signs" and "wonders," are also terms that Paul occasionally uses in tandem with *dynameis* to describe the same phenomenon.[14] *Semeia* points to the divine authority of the events, whereas *terata* emphasizes their unusual quality. Paul does not use *terata* apart from *semeia*, implying that astonishment should not be divorced from theological significance.

The meanings of Paul's words for "miracle" are vague, but he does not suggest that they were disruptions of physical regularities. William Sanday, one of the most respected New Testament exegetes of the past century, maintains that Paul would have shared Augustine's view that miracles are not contrary to nature. Sanday asserts that Paul's terms for miracles refer to "remarkable spiritual gifts, which included the gifts of healing." In his essay on miracles, Sanday states: "The witness of St. Paul is no doubt the best that we have. That of the rest of the New Testament is not quite so immediate."[15]

There is a distinct difference between the way in which *dynamis* was used by Paul and its usual employment in the first century. Regarding the latter, William Ramsay writes: "The word 'power' (*dynamis*) was technical in the language of religion, superstition, and magic, and was one of the most common and characteristic terms in the language of pagan devotion."[16] To convey his lower valuation of wonder-working gifts, Paul follows his mention of such in 1 Corinthians 12 with his ode to love (*agape*) in 1 Corinthians 13. In the latter he distinguishes faith to do miracles (along with other qualities claimed by some Christians) from the highest expression of Christian ethics.

The term *dynamis* is used by Paul much more often than by any other New Testament writer. For him the superlative demonstration of the "*dynamis* of God" is the gospel.[17] Paul found the implosion of Christ's amazing grace to be God's mightiest work. Grace operates within the depth of alienated personalities, liberating them from destructive tendencies.

There is no mention in Paul's letters of any miracles that, according to the later written Gospels, Jesus is alleged to have performed. This significant fact is rarely pointed out, since most New Testament interpreters are devoted to affirming that the varied writers share the same outlook. How can Paul's silence be explained? Perhaps supernatural feats had not yet been associated with Jesus, or, if they had, he did not find them credible. In the Mediterranean culture, stories of supernatural exploits by religious heroes were commonplace, but Paul does not allude to them. He accepted the advice he gave to the Thessalonians, to "test everything," so he did not accept fantastic claims uncritically.[18] Paul may have been aware of some faith healings involving Jesus, but he regarded them as insignificant in comparison to Jesus' embodiment of *agape*. In 1 Corinthians 1:22-24, Paul disparagingly acknowledged that most Jews wanted a miracle-man messiah—perhaps a new Moses or Elijah. In contrast to that longing, the apostle affirms

Christ Jesus as the true *"dynamis* of God." That "miracle" was "scandalous" to many, he admits, because it portrays one who does not supernaturally overcome those who will crucify him. For Paul, however, the wonder-working of God is not displayed in erratic spectaculars, but in Jesus' suffering humanity.

The natural order is dependable enough for Paul to draw a parallel between predictability in the physical and moral realms. Just as a farmer generally reaps in accord to how he plants, so divine judgment operates through consequential causality.[19] According to Paul, individuals who are alienated from God reap in their personalities the natural, disintegrating consequences.[20]

Paul found at the heart of Christianity a transformation of values. In popular religion, people commonly expect to experience the divine in supernatural occurrences. Had Jesus been one more thaumaturge, he would not have been revolutionary. There were shamans and wizards galore in folk culture. Indeed, in Jesus' day, as Gerd Theissen documents in his excellent recent book on miracles, there was "a renaissance of belief in miracles."[21] But Paul paradoxically found potency in what was commonly regarded as impotent. He revered a modest person who, like Stephen, died loving those who persecuted him.[22] Paul was convinced that God chooses the weak and despised, not those who are strong by ordinary standards.[23] His model of true humanity is a second Adam who, unlike the first, steadfastly lives in humble obedience to God.[24] Paul's Jesus transformed religious expectations by showing that God's action is best seen in situations of lowly oppression, not lofty splendor. "The word of the cross is foolishness to those who are perishing," Paul claims, "but to us who are being saved it is the *dynamis* of God."[25]

It is instructive to piece together what Paul says about the historic Jesus. What he excludes may be as significant as what he includes. Far from endorsing an unnatural, virginal conception, he refers to "the Son of God" as simply "from David's seed" and "born of woman, born under the law."[26] The miracle of Jesus' life pertains to values rather than to biology: though he was "rich" he became "poor" through self-giving.[27] "Not counting equality with God a thing to be grasped, he emptied himself, taking the form of a servant."[28] The apostle appeals to Christians "on the basis of the gentleness and kindness of Christ."[29] Paul's Jesus taught about human relationships and lived an exemplary life.[30] In relation to God, he is the unique elder brother amid a human family circle of many sons and daughters.[31] Paul's Jesus was not a miracle worker who attempted to gain the confidence of people by unnatural performances. He acted contrary to establishment morality, but not contrary to established physical regularities. There is no evidence that Paul thought of Jesus as one who could suspend the force of gravity, manipulate the elements to change water to wine, or reverse the putrefaction of a corpse. After a life of loving service, Jesus presided "on the night when he was betrayed" over a supper with his disciples. Manna was not provided from heaven nor was the wine transubstantiated; on the contrary, natural food and drink was consumed.[32]

Paul was aware of unworthy leaders who claimed they were accompanied by "signs and wonders,"[33] so an attempt to prove the preeminence of Jesus by appeal to similar phenomena would be of little value.[34] Those who pretend to engage in supernatural sorcery are judged by Paul as lacking "the fruits of the Spirit."[35] Practitioners of magic arts are motivated by a love of power that blinds them to the self-authenticating power of *agape*.

Paul's general disdainful outlook on supernaturalism provides a clue for understanding the position of those Jewish Christians whom he sarcastically labels "superapostles."[36] He indicates that those adversaries, whom he encountered in Corinth, featured "signs and wonders" to legitimize their status, and he accuses them of preaching about "another Jesus."[37] "This other Jesus," James Robinson suggests, "is a power-laden glorious miracle worker."[38] Dieter Georgi argues that those opponents of Paul imitated a propaganda tactic used by Jewish missionaries in Diaspora synagogues.[39] The opponents probably treated Jesus as one who performed wonders similar to those of some prophets recorded in the Old Testament. Georgi also maintains that Paul's adversaries arrogantly presumed they could perform mighty works like those ascribed to Moses, Elijah, and Jesus.[40] A study by John Gager shows that Moses was the most popular Jewish figure in the Hellenistic culture because "his status as a powerful magician was exalted" by Jewish spokesmen.[41] Paul strongly resists those who smugly thought they were more evangelical because they stressed marvelous acts that were being attributed to Jesus. The apostle focuses on "the glory of God in the face of Christ"[42] and does not try to find that glory shining through miracles which Jesus may have performed. Moreover, in his Corinthians correspondence, Paul depreciates the haloed Moses who charmed Hellenistic Judaism. Although a principal figure in what Paul designates the "old covenant," Moses has a "fading splendor."[43]

Paul's Corinthian opponents have interested Helmut Koester, Harvard's leading New Testament scholar. In analyzing their position, he writes: "Paul realized that the emphasis upon the supernatural elements denigrates the normal human experiences, because divine presence is not found in the common, everyday occurrences, events, actions, and tribulations of men. Thus there is no continuity of faith and life with the earthly, human Jesus."[44] Ernst and Marie-Luise Keller, in one of the best treatments of New Testament miracles, correctly assert that Paul was "not interested in physical miracles; they do not fit into the picture which he gives of the earthly Jesus, and they are meaningless for the Christology that he preaches."[45]

The Gospel of Mark

The four Gospels, dating from about A.D. 75-95, inconsistently blend traditions of a suffering and a supernatural Jesus. The passion of Jesus is set forth in the latter portion of Mark, in accordance with the teachings of Paul. Jesus is not pictured there as a superman who tears himself from his cross to frustrate his revilers.[46] On the other hand, several chapters of Mark do portray Jesus with superhuman powers. If references to miraculous happenings were cut out of Paul's letters, only a few verses would be lost: similar surgery on Mark would remove one-third of the Gospel.

The Gospel writers evidently appreciated the approach of the "superapostles" whom Paul satirized. Dennis Duling discerns a basic contrast between Paul's letters and the Gospels, the two main portions of the New Testament: "Paul opposed the divine man approach to Jesus Christ, in which Jesus was pictured as a spirit-filled miracle worker.... Studies of the Gospels indicate that Mark and John had at their disposal collections of miracle stories about Jesus."[47] In a painstaking literary analysis, Paul Achtemeier reveals a parallel "pre-Marcan miracle catenae" in Mark 4:35-6:44 and 6:45-8:10. He maintains that "the groups which formed the catenae drew from those traditions in ways similar to those in which Paul's opponents in Corinth drew upon them."[48] Here we have a fundamental inconsistency in the outlook on supernaturalism of New Testament writers. J. Christiaan Beker, in his recent comprehensive treatment of Paul's theology, exclaims: "It seems as if the Corinthians base their theology on the 'superman Jesus' of Mark 3-9 or his miracle source and omit Mark's passion story!"[49]

Why did some early Christians tell of a superman Jesus if, in fact, the historical Jesus functioned as an inspiring leader, an enlightening teacher, and a compassionate physician? The Gospel writers seem determined to demonstrate how the founder of Christianity is as spectacular as any of the acclaimed Jewish and pagan wonder-workers. This intention is not made explicit and is probably not fully conscious and deliberate. In Judaism the prophets Moses, Elijah, and Elisha were the ones most associated with extraordinary feats. Moses is remembered as one who, as Yahweh's agent, controlled a sea in order to accomplish the Israelite exodus.[50] Jewish lore contains echoes of Moses' power over waters that hinder people. According to the Scriptures, the cloak of Elijah was powerful enough to divide the Jordan River twice, enabling Elijah and Elisha to walk to the east side together and then helping Elisha to return conveniently.[51] Centuries later Rabbis Gamaliel and Tanchuma, at different times, were at sea when a tempest threatened to sink their boats. After they prayed the waters immediately quieted down.[52] In a similar manner Mark's Jesus calms a sea so his disciples can cross to the other side.[53]

From the beginning of Mark onward, John the Baptist is portrayed as being to Jesus what Elijah was to Elisha. Dressed with a leather belt over his haircloth, Elijah denounced his king and queen and commissioned at the Jordan River one who was eager to obtain the prophet's spirit.[54] John likewise, wearing the same rough clothing, condemns the wickedness of his king and queen. He encounters his successor at the Jordan and initiates him into a Spirit-filled ministry.[55] According to Jewish reckoning, Elisha performed sixteen miracles after receiving the Spirit.[56] Mark's Jesus also performs sixteen miracles[57] and some are quite similar. In one story Elisha takes a small amount of food and divides it among a number of people, and has some left after everyone was fed. A parallel incident in Mark is the two multitude feedings, except that Mark shows Jesus feeding more people with less than the original quantity of food.[58] Again, like Elisha, Jesus gains fame by curing a leper, and both miraculously open blind eyes.[59] Stories were told of both Elijah and Elisha shutting themselves up with young persons who had died and then restoring them to life.[60]

Accordingly, Mark's Jesus, after arranging for privacy, restored a dead youth; after this act some Jews concluded that Elijah had returned in the person of Jesus.[61]

A fundamental difference between Paul's Jesus and Mark's Jesus is apparent. The latter fulfilled a popular Jewish expectation that a wonder-working Israelite prophet redivivus would establish the messianic era. Jesus ben Sirach, two centuries before the Christian era, had written about one who would come "at the appointed time": "How glorious you were, Elijah, in your miracles! Who else can boast of such deeds? You raised a corpse from death."[62] Unlike Mark and the other Gospels, Paul never suggests Jesus is a new Elijah or Elisha. In his only reference to either prophet, the apostle recalls Elijah's feelings of weakness and loneliness.[63] Thus, even if Paul had conceived of Jesus as a new Elijah, attention probably would have been given to Elijah's suffering role rather than to his herculean exploits.

In contrast to early Christians with a Jewish background, some Gentile Christians transferred pagan motifs of unnatural wonders to Jesus. Greek thaumaturges are a common feature in the hero cults of late antiquity.[64] Before the beginning of the Christian era, legends attribute philosopher Empedocles with the power to resurrect the dead and arrest violent wind.[65] Christian theologian Justin Martyr in the second century acknowledges a similarity between the powers of Asclepius and Jesus. He writes: "When we say that Jesus healed the lame, the paralytic, and those born blind, and raised the dead, we seem to be talking about things like those said to have been done by Asclepius."[66] In the third century, a biography of Pythagoras by Porphyry contains teachings along with a collection of miracle stories, not unlike the Gospel accounts. The biography alleges that the power of Pythagoras' word could stop earthquakes and calm tempestuous seas. Whereas Mark's Jesus was seen "walking on the sea,"[67] Porphyry's Pythagoras "crossed rivers and seas and impassable places, somehow walking in the air."[68] These tales may have been influenced by stories from India which were becoming known in the Mediterranean region at the time. Sanskrit scholar William Brown observes: "Walking on the water is recognized in India as one of the stages of the psychic power of levitation, of which the highest grade is flying through the air. Levitation is very old in Hindu literature, appearing in *Rigveda* 10, 136, and therefore being from before 800 B.C."[69]

As widely recognized, the literature with the closest parallels to the Gospel genre is Philostratus' life of Apollonius. This biography, recorded in the third century but based on earlier sources, states that a miracle accompanied the birth of Apollonius when he was born during the reign of Caesar Augustus.[70] After studying Pythagorean lore, he travelled from town to town, teaching and performing miracles. He ministered to a boy possessed by an alien spirit, restored a blind man, cured a man with a paralyzed arm, and ascended bodily into heaven after his own death.[71]

Latin authors who were contemporaries of Jesus report that an amazing diagnosis of Asclepiades saved a person from premature burial. "When he met a funeral procession," Celsus records, "he recognized that a man who was being carried out to burial was alive."[72] Similar discernment is associated with Jesus in Mark's Gospel. He encounters funeral mourners weeping over Jairus' daughter whom they presume has just died. They do not believe Jesus when he assures them the girl is comatose, but not dead. After he takes her hand and tells her to arise, she revives.[73]

About the time the Gospel of Mark was written Vespasian was claimed to have performed miracles in Alexandria to authenticate his sovereignty. Both Tacitus and Suetonius report that the Roman emperor instantly healed a lame man and, after applying his spittle to defective eyes, cured a blind man.[74] The saliva treatment used by Vespasian on his visit to Egypt had been long associated in that country with magic.

For example, the Pyramid Texts state that Thoth healed Horus' eye by spitting on it. Strikingly similar to these accounts of Egyptian cures is the claim in Mark 8:23 that Jesus removed impediments to sight by spitting on the eyes of a blind man. After dealing thoroughly with this and other examples of magic in Mark, John Hull concludes: "By the time the earliest gospel was written the tradition of the acts of Jesus had already become saturated with the outlook of Hellenistic magic."[75]

Mark's Jesus teaches that "all things are possible to him who believes,"[76] but Paul testifies that persistent prayer did not effect a cure for his personal suffering. Rather, he found that his faith enabled him to cope with, but not remove, "weaknesses, insults, hardships, persecutions, and calamities."[77] One passage in Mark is especially incongruous with Paul's outlook. Mark's Jesus acts to destroy life and then to teach that uncritical belief can accomplish the most absurd natural impossibilities imaginable. According to Mark, Jesus was irritated on finding a fig tree without fruit on it for him to eat. Since figs ripen in Palestine during the summer, it was irrational for him to expect to find any at the Passover season in the springtime. Mark acknowledges that only leaves were on the tree "for it was not the season for figs." Although in no way the tree's fault, Jesus, out of selfish anger, issues this curse: "May no one ever eat fruit from you again." Assuming animism, the bizarre story says the hexed tree "withered away to its roots" before the next day. Jesus then comments on the capricious efficacy of magic:

> Have faith in God. Truly, I say to you, whoever says to this mountain, "Be taken up and cast into the sea," and does not doubt it in his heart, but believes that what he says will come to pass, it will be done for him. Therefore I tell you, whatever you ask in prayer, believe that you receive it, and you will.[78]

Paul would surely have found it out of character for Jesus to blast God's creative activity when fruit was not provided out of season, or to recommend praying for a supernatural catastrophe to achieve any whim one might have. The apostle places a zero value on such arbitrary unloving attitudes when he posed this hypothetical hyperbole: "If I have all faith, so as to remove mountains, but have not love, I am nothing."[79] The Jesus whom Paul follows fulfills Isaiah's prophesy of a coming servant of the Lord who figuratively would "not break a bruised reed." The humble sufferer would express no vengeance or selfishness; he would not condemn a fruit tree—literal or symbolic—that was just awakening from dormancy to produce fruit in due season.[80]

Several stages in the miracle growth within the New Testament are unfolding. Paul's Jesus is mainly an enfleshment of holy, suffering *agape*. Mark's Jesus is all of this plus a somewhat limited supernatural thaumaturge. The Jesus of each of the later Gospels has even fewer human limitations. Most Christians do not recognize the disparate strands in the tangled skein of New Testament literature, so they presume that all sectors of the early church believed the founder of Christianity performed miracles to prove his divine qualities.

Other Gospels and Acts

There is a scholarly consensus that Matthew and Luke were written approximately a decade after Mark and about half a century after Jesus' public ministry. The later Synoptic Gospels borrow heavily from Mark and occasionally heighten the supernaturalism that it contains. Theissen, by scrutinizing the Gospel miracles, found seventeen instances where the miraculous is enlarged in the transmission from Mark to Matthew.[81] Those changes were made in the effort to portray Jesus as the majestic Lord who has been given "all power in heaven and on earth."[82] In Matthew's account, for example, the fig tree

withers "immediately" after Jesus curses it.[83] In one of Mark's
stories Jairus tells Jesus his daughter is dying and requests she
be healed; but in Matthew, Jairus states she has died and
requests that she be resurrected.[84] Embellishment may also be
detected in a miracle performed at Jericho, for Matthew dou-
bles the number of people whose sight is restored.[85]

Of all the New Testament writers, Luke is the most fascinated with wonder-workers. This characteristic is revealed to a
lesser extent in his Gospel narrative and to a greater extent in
his Acts of the Apostles. Luke compares the beginning of
Jesus' public ministry with Elijah's, who assisted a Sidonian
widow, and with Elisha's, who cleansed a leper.[86] Elijah miraculously supplied food for the woman and revived her dead
son.[87] Luke's Jesus, as a greater Elijah, miraculously feeds a
multitude and raises two youth from the dead, one being a
widow's son.[88] In addition, he cures at least ten more Gentile
lepers than Elisha.[89] Luke occasionally adds miracles to the
stories he obtained from Mark's Gospel. Luke states that Jesus
told Peter to cast out his nets again at a time when the fisher-
man was convinced no fish were around. When Peter followed
Jesus' instructions, the nets began to break because of the
enormous catch and the boat began to sink.[90] Again, according
to Mark, one of Jesus' disciples cut off an ear of the high
priest's slave in the Garden of Gethsemane. Luke adds that
Jesus "touched his ear and healed him."[91] After discussing
differences in other miracle stories among the synoptic Gospels, Achtemeier concludes:

> Of all the gospels, Luke appears to have a more unambiguous
> reliance on the possibility that miracles, and thus miracle-
> stories, can serve as the basis for faith in Jesus.... Luke seems to
> view the miracles with a less critical eye, according them, in a
> number of subtle ways, a more important role in his account of
> Jesus. A glance at Acts confirms that impression and shows the
> extent to which Luke understood the miraculous to play an

important, if not, indeed, a central role, in the origins of the Christian church.[92]

As Luke started on his second scroll concerning the beginnings of Christianity, his imagination was probably stimulated by ascension claims in earlier legends. It is likely that he shared with his contemporary Plutarch an awareness of the well-known story of Romulus, which claimed the body of Rome's founder disappeared without a trace and ascended to heaven. Plutarch also cites tales of the vanished corpses of other prominent men. That Greek writer, who is skeptical of such stories, suggests that they "are told by writers who improbably deify the mortal part of human nature along with the divine."[93] Also, Luke may have known that a Roman official swore he had seen the form of Augustus rise above the emperor's funeral pyre "on its way to heaven."[94] Justin not only alludes to the account of that deified Roman but also points out that the story of Jesus' ascension is similar to tales told about Asclepius, Bacchus, Hercules, Romulus, and other heroes.[95]

Several parallels may be drawn between the final Elijah story and the final story of Luke's resurrected Jesus. When Elijah died, according to the Jewish Scriptures, he had a unique ascension into the sky, which was accompanied by fire from heaven and a large outpouring of his spirit on his successor, Elisha.[96] Accordingly, Jesus' crucified body was raised to heaven and soon afterwards his disciples beheld tongues like fire from heaven while they became filled with the Holy Spirit.[97]

One outward manifestation of the Spirit-experience is "speaking in tongues." Luke interprets glossolalia as a miraculous ability to communicate in foreign languages, whereas Paul treats it as ecstatic babbling, devoid of intellectual content.[98] The sermon on that day of Pentecost focuses on "Jesus of Nazareth, a man attested to you by God with mighty works and wonders and signs."[99] Luke may be given the dubious

distinction of being the first apologist to attempt to prove
Jesus' messiahship and godliness by his alleged miracles.

Another expression of Spirit activity in Acts is a continuation of miracles similar to some Luke wrote about on his first
scroll. The curing of a cripple by Peter and John in Acts 3
resembles the healing of the paralytic in Luke 5, and the raising
of Tabitha by Peter in Acts 9 parallels the raising of Jairus'
daughter in Luke 8. Here again Luke patterns his account on
the Elijah-Elisha saga. In his doctoral dissertation, Marvin
Miller analyzes these Luke-Acts stories and concludes: "The
intention of Luke is fairly clear; the miracles of the disciples
approximate and continue those of Jesus, just as those of
Elisha did Elijah's."[100]

Judging from the stories in Acts, the performance of wonders is for Luke the *sine qua non* of apostleship and messiahship. He believes such works legitimize status only if they were
inspired by what he identifies as the Holy Spirit. Consequently, a magician named Simon who lacked this Spirit was
not acceptable, even though he was acclaimed "the *dynamis* of
God which is called Great."[101] Peter surpasses the dazzling
reputation of Simon by instantly healing a man who had been
bedridden for years with paralysis and by raising a woman who
had died.[102] Paul is the only apostle who, in Luke's opinion,
can hold his own in miracle competition with Peter. Both heal
men with the same life-long deformity. Even though both men
had been crippled from birth they responded by leaping up and
walking on command of the apostles.[103] Also, Paul once demonstrated his power to restore a dead person to life.[104]

Luke's stories of Paul are more revealing than his stories of
other apostles because they can be compared with factual
activities recorded decades earlier in Paul's letters. A case in
point is the contrasting accounts of Paul's imprisonment situations. Luke portrays Paul as released from the Philippian
prison by an earthquake, which parallels nicely an earlier
account in Acts of Peter's prison break through divine inter-

vention. In the Philippian letter, however, Paul neither alludes
to a previous spectacular prison escape at Philippi nor suggests
that God might use extraordinary means to deliver him from
his present imprisonment.

Ernst Haenchen, in his illuminating Acts commentary,
points out that a primary discrepancy between Luke's Paul
and the epistolary Paul is Luke's portrayal of Paul as a great
miracle worker. Haenchen observes: "It is true that the real
Paul did on one occasion lay claim to the 'signs of an apostle' (2
Cor. 12:12) but the exploits in question were so little out of the
ordinary that his opponents flatly denied his ability to perform
miracles."[105] In his doctoral dissertation, Hisao Kayama likewise exposes this contradiction: "The image of Paul portrayed
by Luke materially coincides with what the opponents accused
Paul of lacking."[106] Luke certainly does not picture Paul as the
apostle viewed himself, a weak instrument of God who could
not overcome obstacles by feats of supernaturalism, even if he
had so desired. The *dynamis* of Paul, like that of his crucified
Lord, was displayed in ways considered foolish in ancient
religions.

Luke's Paul is first shown to excel over rival religionists even
as Moses triumphed over Egyptian magicians.[107] When Ely-
mas, a Jewish magician, opposed Paul in Cyprus, the missionary cast a spell on him which immediately caused blindness.
Luke, thinking the miracle is the message, presumed that this
astounding magic caused a Roman proconsul to "believe."[108]

Although there is no reference in Paul's letters to Christians
engaging in exorcism, Luke's Paul is an extraordinary exor-
cist. In Philippi he was confronted by a slave girl who was
possessed by "a python spirit." In the mythology of her Greek
culture a dragon lurked in a cave near Delphi and some associated it with a snake-induced mania. Similar to the way the
priests at the Delphi oracle valued demons as diamonds, the
girl's owners profited on her proclamations during demonic
seizures. But Paul, finding the girl annoying, cast out her

serpentine demon by this incantation: "I charge you in the name of Jesus to come out of her."[109] Later that formula was so effective at Ephesus that some rival exorcists adopted it, but found the results terrible. Luke relates that Paul's touch was so potent he could place a charge on handkerchiefs. When the blessed cloths were carried away from his body to the sick, "diseases left them and the evil spirits came out of them."[110] In Luke's stories, Paul's therapeutic technique is even more fantastic than those of the Gospels' Jesus. Paul's healings were accomplished by fetish cloths containing impersonal mana, whereas Jesus' healings resulted from a one-to-one personal encounter.

One of the last wonder stories in Acts provides fulfillment for words that Luke attributed to Jesus. To his disciples he declares, "I have given you authority to tread upon serpents and scorpions, and over all the power of the enemy; and nothing shall hurt you."[111] Accordingly, after a viper bit Paul on the island of Malta, he cast it into a bonfire. When he did not swell up or drop dead, as the Maltese had expected, they asserted that he was a god.[112] This tale is similar to one told of Rabbi Hanina ben Dosa, who lived at the time of Luke. After being bitten by a poisonous snake, it was the reptile that died.[113] Saintly people were presumed to be immune from snake venom.

Each Gospel writer tells of some stupendous acts by Jesus not found in any other Gospels. The Gospel of John contains a raising-from-the-dead tale that is even more incredible than those reported in the earlier Gospels, for Lazarus had been buried for days and his corpse was putrid.[114] Also, the writer of that Gospel apparently adapted a story of Dionysus transforming water to wine.[115] Such folk tales were circulated regarding that Greek god of wine, one of which tells of several large jugs which became filled with wine in his presence.[116]

Koester has this to say about the miracle stories appearing in John as "signs":

> This source is a collection of pieces from the Hellenistic propaganda in which Jesus is proclaimed as divine man.... It is characteristic of religious syncretism...that one of these miracle narratives (the wine miracle at Cana, John 2:1-11) derived its main feature from the cult of Dionysus. The miraculous power of Jesus is even more emphasized in John's Sign Source than in the Marcan parallels. These stories proclaim Jesus as the god who walks the earth. Instead of speaking about God who raised Jesus from the dead, they preach a Jesus with the divine power to call the dead to life from their tombs.[117]

The Gospel of John does not admit, as do the Synoptics,[118] that others have performed wonders like Jesus. After a blind man's sight is restored, he boasts, "Never since the world began has it been heard that any one opened the eyes of a man born blind."[119] The intensification of Jesus'.powers in the miracles of John is described by Theissen in this way: "They are a continuation of God's work of creation (5:17), and indeed surpass it (5:20). They are unique. No one else can perform them (15:24)."[120]

The writer of the Fourth Gospel retells the feeding of the multitude miracle found five times in the Synoptic Gospels, but he alone explicitly compares the account with the Moses saga. John views Jesus as the fulfillment of this forecast by Moses: "The Lord your God will raise up for you a prophet like me from among you."[121] Moses authenticated that he was God's spokesman by performing miracles. For example, he announced that the rebellious followers of Korah would be killed by falling into the earth when it "opens its mouth." Immediately, the ground under those people split asunder and swallowed them up.[122] According to John, the people ask Jesus, "What sign do you do, that we may see, and believe you?"[123] The miraculous feeding of the multitude by Jesus evokes this response: "When the people saw the sign which he had done, they said, 'This is indeed the prophet who is to come into the world!' "[124] Jesus declares he is greater than Moses, who was associated with the miraculous manna. Jesus' people not only feed on the physical bread he provides but also they feed on himself, "the true bread from heaven" that will give eternal life.[125]

The "signs" in the Fourth Gospel also echo the Elisha legends. Water transformation is the first miracle that both Elisha and Jesus perform. The Israelite prophet manipulated water in a magical manner after receiving a double portion of Elijah's spirit while near the Jordan River. Jesus turns water into wine after returning from the Jordan, where he received the Spirit of God when baptized by John, whom some had presumed was a new Elijah.[126] Then Elisha and Jesus restore a son to health, and they cure a man by having him wash in a designated place.[127] Both multiply a few barley loaves to feed a large crowd.[128] Elisha's levitation magic in making an iron axe head float is matched by Jesus' walking on water.[129] Elisha was so powerful that even after burial his body could revive a corpse.[130] Likewise, the resurrecting of a buried body is Jesus' final miracle, according to the Gospel of John.[131]

Johannine authority Raymond Brown observes that there are closer similarities between the miracles of Jesus and Elisha than between Jesus and any miracle man of Gentile Hellenism.[132] The Jesus of the Fourth Gospel has some of the same qualities which made Elisha highly esteemed in Hellenistic Judaism. Indeed, the Johannine Jesus reflects what Sirach writes of Elisha: "Nothing was too difficult for him; even in death his body kept its prophetic power. In life he worked miracles, and in death his deeds were marvelous."[133]

Post-Biblical Developments

The embellishments on the figures of Jesus and his apostles in some of the New Testament writings, are mild in contrast to stories from the second and later centuries which comprise the New Testament Apocrypha. Luke's treatment of the boyhood of Jesus looks like a model of scholarly discrimination when compared with the fiction contained in the Infancy Gospel of Thomas. Its fabrications come close to misrepresenting completely Luke's record of Jesus' youth. For example, while he was making clay birds out of mud and then giving them life, another boy drained off his mud puddle. Jesus became enraged and pronounced a curse: " 'You shall wither like a tree and shall bear neither leaves, nor root, nor fruit.' Immediately that youth withered up completely." Again, when irritated by a boy who brushed against him, revengeful Jesus said words that caused the boy to drop dead. In another instance, Jesus assisted in Joseph's carpentry shop by creating out of nothing additional length for boards that were too short.[134]

Some of the miracle stories about Jesus claim to be based on information received from his mother. She informed church leaders Timothy and Theophilus in Egypt that, while her family lived there, Jesus turned camels into stones and caused idol temples to collapse. By making a sign with his little hand, a chariot was shattered, killing a magician and her daughter. When Jesus stuck Joseph's olivewood cane in the ground, it immediately grew branches and bore fruit. Once Mary, Joseph, and Jesus wished to travel by boat, when winds were so turbulent that the sailors refused to take them aboard. Jesus responded not only by stilling the storm but also by causing a rock on which his family was waiting to move across the water, carrying them to their destination.[135]

The license taken with the apostles' lives in the New Testament Apocrypha was no doubt encouraged by the Acts of the Apostles. Luke alleges in Acts, as we have seen, that some of the apostles continued to perform miracles as spectacular as those which Jesus performed. Accordingly, in the apocryphal acts of the apostles mass healings occur and a number of people are raised from the dead. The canonical Acts asserts that the sick were placed in the Jerusalem streets with hopes that at least Peter's shadow would fall on them. It is stated that all of them were healed.[136] This story is more than matched in the apocryphal acts, in an account of Peter praying for the healing of some blind widows. In response, a light flashes that restores their sight. Peter also took a smoked fish hanging in a market and said, "If you now see this swimming in the water like a fish, will you be able to believe in him whom I preach?" On receiving an affirmative reply, Peter threw the fish in a pond. The fish came back to life and many converted to Christianity because of the supernatural display.[137]

The supernaturalism associated with Paul is also spectacular. He saved a companion from being burned alive by efficaciously praying for rain to extinguish the pyre.[138] Not only did Peter raise people from the dead but also Paul resurrected a boy in Antioch, a man called Dion in Myra, and a woman named Frontina who had been thrown from a rock.[139] In addition, claims were made that two persons were raised from the dead by Thomas, and four by John.[140]

Animals become harmless to Christians in the apocryphal acts. Beasts in the arena refuse to attack the bodies of martyrs.[141] Bed-bugs leave the room when the apostle John requests: "I tell you, you bugs, to behave yourselves, one and all; you must leave your home for tonight and be quiet in one place and keep your distance from the servants of God."[142] Many Christians in the early church apparently had an insatiable appetite for astounding miracle stories.

The Acts of John also extends the notion that Jesus' body was not subject to the force of gravity. Not only did he walk on the surface of the sea without sinking but he also never made a footprint when he moved about on land.[143] Jesus is here viewed more as an angel or a phantom than as a person with physical substance.

Gregory of Nyssa, a distinguished fourth century Greek bishop, moved the defense of Christianity down an irrational *cul de sac* when he argued that "the evidence for Jesus' divinity comes through his miracles."[144] Recognizing the competition in this field, Gregory made this special plea for Jesus: "His walking through the sea was different from Moses' sea miracle that separated waters on either side and made bare its depth for those who passed through, for the surface of the water provided solid support for his feet."[145]

Emphasis on miracles was as prominent in the Latin Church as in the Greek Church. For example, Pope Gregory the Great believed that in the Middle Ages miracles were still happening like those alleged in the Bible. He tells of one monk who brought a boy back to life and of another one who ran on the surface of water.[146] Bishop Fortunatus raised Marcellus, who had been dead for a day, and two nuns left the tombs where they had been interred.[147] Gregory relates a tale pertaining to a Roman official who suddenly died after seducing a virgin. After he was buried, an infernal fire issued forth from his grave, consuming his corpse.[148] Benedicta Ward has described the way belief in miracles occupied a major part of the medieval outlook.[149] Post-biblical miracles were thought by Catholic Christians to reinforce ancient testimony to the omnipotence of the Judeo-Christian God. Bizarre miracles were attributed to the relics of saints. The literature of the Middle Ages was full of stories of saints who "could prophesy the future, control the weather, provide protection against fire and flood, magically transport heavy objects, and bring relief to the sick." Church buildings displayed the orientation toward magic, for bells were placed on them not so much to notify the congregation as to dispel the demons.[150]

Miracles have had a place in Christian apologetics even in the post-Renaissance era. As we have seen, Francis Xavier was accorded a host of miracles in seventeenth century Catholicism. The Vatican Council in 1870 reaffirmed that the divine origin of Christianity can be proved by miracles. Anglican Alan Richardson probably expresses the position of most contemporary Christians when he asserts that the supernaturalism of the Gospel is a necessary "authentication of the divine mission of Jesus."[151]

Historical Observations on Miracles

Oxford professor Matthew Arnold writes: "It is almost impossible to exaggerate the proneness of the human mind to take miracles as evidence, and to seek for miracles as evidence: or the extent to which religion...is still held in connection with a reliance upon miracles."[152] Russian novelist Fyodor Dostoevsky comments: "Man'seeks not so much God as the miraculous. And as man cannot bear to be without the miraculous, he will create new miracles of his own for himself, and will worship deeds of sorcery and witchcraft."[153]

In this examination of the growth of the miraculous in Christianity, we have seen an obvious increase not only between the canonical and the apocryphal New Testament but also within the crucial first century. Students of Christian origins are aware of the former growth, but few admit the most rapid inflation occurred during the decades the New Testament books were being written. The fact that the sequence of the traditional arrangement of those books is not related to the date of composition has made it difficult for some to perceive the striking growth of supernaturalism during the latter half of the first century.

Some scholars wrongly presume that the Gospel stories about Jesus' miracles accurately represent Jesus' own outlook. Morton Smith, for example, in *Jesus the Magician*, disregards the earliest information about Jesus in the New Testament and concentrates on the four Gospels. Smith does not take into account the humiliation role that Paul's letters report Jesus to have experienced. Therefore Smith holds that "Jesus won his following primarily as a miracle worker."[154] Smith's thesis is unsound because he does not consider what was recorded about Jesus decades before the Gospels were written. The extensive Quelle ("Q") source, the scholarly designation of material quoted by both Matthew and Luke, combines with Paul's letters to show clearly that Jesus was not remembered mainly because of his miracles. Whoever compiled "Q" was principally concerned with the teachings of Jesus, as the "Sermon on the Mount" illustrates.

Obviously a true understanding of a historical person must begin with a study of the earliest relevant records. The figure of Jesus is less likely distorted by Paul in his correspondence than by the sermons about Jesus that later constituted the Gospels. The fact that Paul says nothing about Jesus as a miracle worker is important, especially since Paul believes Jesus embodied the most godlike qualities. The apostle realizes that a being who does not share our natural limitations cannot be fully incarnate. Paul does not share the gnostic dualism that attempts to superimpose a spiritual nature on a human nature. All authentic portraits of Jesus must rely upon Paul's brief but telling sketch of his Jewish contemporary.

Further understanding of literary developments in Christianity may be gained by examining parallel situations in other world religions that originated in Asia. Zoroasterianism, Buddhism, and Islam have in their traditions a growth of miracles attributed to their founders. In the *Gathas*, the only source for information about the historical Zoroaster, there is no suggestion of miraculous powers. However, legends of such infiltrated the tradition later, including his "confining of hail, spiders, locusts, and other terrors."[155] The historical Buddha reacted negatively to the levitation claims of those in his traditional religion. Gautama taught: "There is no path through the air; one does not become a holy man by outward acts."[156] Although he approved of "the miracle of instruction," he judged appeals to supernaturalism as devoid of spiritual significance as conjurers' tricks. In one story Gautama meets an ascetic who claims he can cross a river by walking on water. The Buddha judges walking on water a waste of effort because riding a ferry is inexpensive. In spite of Buddha's distaste for the miraculous, incredible legends arose regarding his ability to vanish and reappear, to pass through walls, and to fly like an eagle.[157] In the *Koran*, Mohammed affirms that the performance of signs and wonders are not a part of his mission, and he criticizes those who demand such. To that prophet the superlative wonder is the internal revelation that God has given his messengers across the centuries. Even though Mohammed repeatedly disclaimed miraculous powers, supernatural feats began to be told of him after his death. Included in the lore is an account of Mohammed displaying his power over nature by having trees move at his command to provide himself shade, and by multiplying one family's dinner to feed a multitude.[158]

Despite the scientific revolution of modern history, a vast number of Christians still believe that the more contrary an event is to the natural pattern, the greater the religious value. A survey taken in the United States during the past generation indicates that 50% of the Protestants and 71% of the Roman Catholics believe the statement "Jesus walked on water" is "completely true."[159] The emphasis of much of the "electronic religion" that permeates the air waves is on supernaturalism. It is smug to presume that all ancient people were uncritical of supernaturalism or that modern scientific understanding is rapidly dispelling all miracle mania. In every century some people are skeptical of alleged miracles and others are credulous. Cicero, a Roman statesman with religious convictions who lived before Paul, reasons: "Nothing can happen without cause; nothing happens that cannot happen, and when what was capable of happening has happened, it may not be interpreted as a miracle. Consequently, there are no miracles."[160] Paul, like Plutarch, Polybius, and Herodotus,[161] is cautious in accepting accounts widely believed by the simple. If many of the uneducated people in ancient times believed a person could walk on water, no doubt some of the sophisticated among them questioned it—suggesting possible explanations such as hallucination, or frozen water, or stepping stones at the surface. Had Paul encountered someone walking on water, he would more likely have asked, "How do you do that?" than have declared, "You must be divine." It is only a modern prejudice to assume that ancient people had no concept of natural regularity. On the other hand, in our so-called scientific age, many people are duped by tales of the Bermuda triangle, the Loch Ness monster, chariots of extraterrestrial gods, and by seances offering afterlife data.

Christians have often not been as perceptive as some of their prominent antagonists who recognized that one more wonder-working cult leader was nothing momentous. On the contrary, such a person was presumed to be deceptive, and his stature was diminished among those who respected the created natural order. Trypho, a Jewish opponent in the second century, believed Christianity is centered in "a magician who led the people astray."[162] Celsus, a Platonist, shortly afterwards wrote a treatise attacking Christianity, in part because "it was by magic that Jesus was able to do the miracles which he performed."[163] Celsus held that Jesus learned his tricks from the Egyptians.[164] In the fourth century, Emperor Julian was willing to grant that Jesus "surpassed all the magicians and charlatans of every place and every time." Even though that Roman acknowledged that Jesus "walked on the sea and drove out demons," he judged that "during his lifetime he accomplished nothing worth hearing of."[165] Classicist E.R. Dodds points out that "miracles were both commonplace and morally suspect" in late antiquity.[166] While opponents of Christianity generally did not deny grand miracles to Jesus, they regarded them as "full of sound and fury, signifying nothing."

Dostoevsky, as we have noted, is fully aware of the human obsession with those who claim to be able to suspend natural causality. He portrays that bent in order to set in bolder relief the intention of the founder of Christianity. In the Grand Inquisitor passage, Dostoevsky expresses a trenchant understanding of Jesus: "You did not want to bring man to you by miracles, because you wanted their freely given love rather than the servile rapture of slaves subdued forever by a display of power." This summing up of Jesus' values was drawn from selected portions of the New Testament. The Jesus of Paul's letter is awesome not because he intervenes in the natural process, but because he inaugurates a community bearing these delectable "fruits of the Spirit": "love, joy, peace, patience, kindness, goodness, faithfulness, gentleness, and self-control."[167]

2

FROM SEXUAL TO ASEXUAL BIRTH

The longest battle of Christian supernaturalists has been with reductive naturalists over the means by which Jesus was born. The supernaturalists believe Jesus was not conceived as other humans by the union of the sperm of a man with the ovum of a woman. Rather, he was conceived when the Spirit of God acted miraculously in the uterus of a girl who had never experienced sexual intercourse. On the other hand, the naturalists maintain that sperm is necessary for all human reproduction and therefore, if Jesus was really human, he must have been conceived by sexual union. For the naturalist any reference to God in explaining biological processes is irrelevant. Both parties of this dispute have fallen into the fallacy of false disjunction. Seldom heard is a third position, that may be

45

designated the position of the religious naturalist. By avoiding an either/or mode of thinking, that viewpoint may be more in line with the thinking of the ancient Hebrews and earliest Christians.

Dual Paternity

The etymology of "procreate" suggests the ancient theology of generation. A *pro*creator is one who acts on behalf of a creator, just as a *pro*noun represents a noun. In ancient cultures it was commonly believed that the Creator works through human procreators in the conception of a baby. Realizing that pregnancy does not occur in most instances of sexual intercourse, they explained fertilization by references to the will of deity and the desire of sexual partners. Giving honor to deity was also a way of evoking humble gratitude for the wonderful gift of new life. Dual paternity is an appropriate label for referring to the divine presence in any human conception that he/she has blessed. The Chinese dual paternity idea can be discerned in this saying of Confucius: "The female alone cannot procreate; the male alone cannot propagate; and Heaven alone cannot produce a man. The three collaborating, man is born. Hence anyone may be called the son of his mother or the son of Heaven."[1] The Egyptians sang to god Aton: "Creator of seed in woman,/ Thou who makest fluid into man,/ Who maintainest the son in the womb of his mother...."[2] These sentiments are attributed to King Ikhnaton, who did not view human and divine paternity as mutually exclusive. "In Egyptian thought," writes Thomas Boslooper, "the natural act of procreation was also an act of God."[3]

In their more mystical moods, the Hebrews thought of a procreative trinity composed of God, husband, and wife. Dual paternity can be found in both ordinary and extraordinary situations in their Scriptures. An illustration of the former is in

Ruth 4:13: "Boaz took Ruth and she became his wife. When he had intercourse with her, the Lord caused her to conceive and she bore a son." The divine presence was considered even more significant when a wife conceived who had been thought barren. The most prominent example of such a situation is found in Genesis 21:1-2: "The Lord visited Sarah as he had said, and the Lord did to Sarah as he had promised. And Sarah conceived, and bore Abraham a son in his old age." This dual paternity is described by John Otwell: "The new life given the people of God came into being because the Lord worked in the woman's womb, bringing to fruition the sexual relations of husband and wife. Thus the woman was uniquely the locus of the basic manifestation of the benign presence of God in the midst of the people, for without new life the people would soon cease to exist."[4]

In some other Hebrew birth accounts the human father is implicitly assumed but not explicitly mentioned. As a way of expressing piety, it is said of Rachel and again of Leah that God "opened her womb."[5] Also, a Hebrew poet, without intending to deny the role of his human father, thought of God as the prime cause of his conception. That psalmist addressed God in this way: "You formed my inward parts;/ You knit me together in my mother's womb."[6]

The sensibility in Scriptures to the agency of God in events is a product not so much of poetic fancy as of theological conviction. The Hebrews, living as they did in a pre-scientific culture, were not awed by physical causation. Although at times they did show an awareness of such, they considered it relatively insignificant in comparison with divine causation. For example, in the Exodus account of the crossing of the Sea of Reeds, there is mention of "a strong east wind" separating the waters. But that explanation is not as important as the affirmation regarding the Lord's action: "At the blast of your nostrils the waters piled up."[7]

As a part of their belief in a continuously creative God, the

Hebrews held that organic life could not be adequately explained in a physiological manner. Acting as a life force was one function of God's Spirit, producing land fertility and animal reproduction as well as human offspring.[8] Job affirms: "The Spirit of God has made me."[9] Accordingly, people were sometimes dignified as "children of the living God."[10]

Ancient Jewish tradition makes more explicit the theory of dual paternity suggested by the Scriptures. Eve's exclamation, "I have brought a child into being with the help of the Lord,"[11] is given this interpretation in the Talmud: "There are three partners in the production of any human being—the Holy One, blessed be He, his father, and his mother."[12] According to Jewish scholar Israel Abraham, "the rabbinic theory of marital intercourse is summed up" in the claim of God's participation as a third parent in every act of procreation.[13] A similar conviction is expressed in a midrash: "In the past Adam was created from the dust of the ground and Eve was created from Adam. Henceforth it is to be 'in our image and after our likeness'— meaning, man will not be able to come into existence without woman, nor woman without man, nor both without the Shekinah."[14] "Shekinah" is a post-biblical circumlocution for Yahweh and is often used interchangeably with "Holy Spirit."[15] It literally means "the One who Dwells Within" and thus refers to the immanent expression of God. The Shekinah is present when the devout assemble to worship[16] and when partners relate to one another in marriage. "When husband and wife are worthy," the Talmud states, "the Shekinah is with them."[17] Thus the Spirit creates when devoted couples pro-create.

Philo, a Jewish contemporary of Jesus, shares the belief of Palestinian rabbis that procreation results from divine-human cooperation.[18] For example, he states that Isaac was a son of Abraham and Sarah[19] and also a "son of God" because he was begotten by God.[20] In one treatise Philo draws allegorical significance from the fact that there is no overt mention of Abraham, Isaac, Jacob, and Moses engaging in marital intercourse. He suggests that this figuratively means the wives of patriarchs were impregnated by God.[21]

It is seen then that ancient Jews in both of the main geographic divisions—from the Diaspora and the Palestinian areas—accepted a theory of dual paternity. No historical data indicates that they believed life could be propagated without human insemination. The ancient Jews viewed pagan legends of unnatural conceptions as blasphemous because they were counter to the Genesis theology of creation. The Hebrews held that the Torah's first command, "Be fruitful and multiply," was obeyed when God's blessing was coupled with the heterosexual union of those made in his image.

New Testament Accounts of Jesus' Birth

What do the earliest historical sources of Christianity say about Jesus' paternity? To emphasize his full identification with his ethnic community in genesis and nurture, Paul describes Jesus as "born of woman, born under the Law."[22] The phrase "born of woman" is a biblical idiom meaning the person shared the human condition[23] and does not imply the apostle believed Jesus was conceived without a male procreator. Paul brought divine and human parentage into juxtaposition: Jesus was born of "David's seed according to the flesh," yet he is designated "Son of God."[24] Since it was through Joseph that the early Christians traced Jesus' descent from David, it would have been nonsense for Paul to claim Jesus was of Davidic descent, yet not a physical son of Joseph. Along with other earliest written records about Jesus—the Gospel of Mark and the "Q" document containing material that Matthew and Luke copied—the letters of Paul do not allude to a virginal conception of Jesus. If such an idea had been transmitted to the writers, they judged it either false or insignificant. According to Paul, all Christians are "sons of God" and are thereby privileged to call God "Daddy" (abba), the same familial title that Jesus used.[25] Also, the apostle affirms that Isaac was "born according to the Spirit" even though he was the son of Abraham and Sarah.[26]

In the Fourth Gospel Jesus is called both "Joseph's son" and "God's only son."[27] That Gospel, along with Paul's letters, accounts for most of the New Testament references to Jesus as "Son of God," but neither hints of a virginal conception. The prologue of John states that each person who receives God has come into being through a cause other than desire of a human father. All "children of God," Jesus included, are "the off-spring of God himself."[28] In the dialogue between Jesus and Nicodemus, the evangelist piquantly depicts the complete life as a combination of birth by the Spirit from above and natural, fleshly conception.[29]

The only New Testament books which appear to state that Jesus was virginally conceived are Matthew and Luke. The opening chapter of the First Gospel, as found in the earliest extant manuscripts from the fourth century, is inconsistent in this testimony, since it is through Joseph that Jesus' genealogy is traced. Moreover, Jesus is referred to in Matthew as "the carpenter's son."[30] This inconsistency can be understood by realizing that Matthew 1:18-25 contains redactions added after the nativity story was first recorded. In a scholarly treatment, Charles Davis demonstrates that the earliest tradition proba-bly contained no reference to virginal conception. He con-cludes that the pre-Matthean story read:

> The engendering of Jesus was in this fashion. When his mother Mary was engaged to Joseph, before they came together she was discovered to be pregnant. Now Joseph, her husband, had decided to divorce her, but after he had reflected upon these things, behold, the angel of the Lord appeared to him through a dream saying: "Joseph, do not be afraid to take Mary as your wife; for that which is begotten in her from the Spirit is holy.

She shall bear a son, and you shall call his name Jesus; for he shall save his people from their sins." Rising from the sleep, Joseph did as the angel of the Lord directed him. He took his wife, and she brought forth a son, and he called his name Jesus.[31]

Dual paternity is assumed in the pre-Matthean account by Jewish Christians, but the role of a human male is explicitly excluded in the expansion now called the Gospel of Matthew. Thus, some years after this nativity tradition was first formed, a doctrine of virginal conception was added. This literary reconstruction harmonizes with Irenaeus' statement that a group of Jewish Christians called Ebionites accepted only the Matthean tradition and did not believe that Jesus was virginally conceived.[32] There is no evidence that the Jews expected a virginally conceived Messiah. One Jew, living in the second century of the Christian era, is represented as expressing this hope: "We all await the Christ who will be a man born of men."[33]

The account of Jesus' virginal conception in the Third Gospel rests on a total of six Greek words in Luke 1:34 and 3:23. Otherwise, the entire writings of Luke would unambiguously support a theory of dual paternity. This is clearly seen in the temple episode during Jesus' boyhood when his mother says to Jesus, "Your father and I have been looking for you anxiously." The boy responds by claiming he was in his "Father's house."[34] Luke does not suggest here, nor is it suggested elsewhere in the New Testament, that Joseph stood *in loco parentis* to Jesus or was merely his legal guardian. Also in Luke's Gospel, citizens of Jesus' hometown question, "Is not this Joseph's son?"[35] Along with these assertions pertaining to Jesus' natural family are frequent references to Jesus as son of the divine Father. Although Jesus called God his Father in all four of the Gospels, he still accepted Joseph as his physical father. Jesus affirmed for himself a primary allegiance he advocated for others. "Do not call any man on earth 'father,'" Jesus urged, "for you have one Father, and he is in heaven."[36]

In Luke 1:34 Mary is represented as inquiring after Gabriel's annunciation, "How shall this be, since I know not a man?" If "since I know not a man" is excluded from the question, Mary's puzzlement pertains to the magnificent destiny forecast in the preceding verses for a peasant's son. Mary was already betrothed to Joseph, so she would unlikely have been bewildered over who might become the agent of impregnation. The question would have been pointless if she was anticipating or was engaging in matrimonial relations with Joseph. A number of New Testament scholars plausibly conjecture that the allusion to virginal conception in Luke 1:34 is an interpolation added to what Luke wrote.[37]

The genealogy of Jesus in Luke 3:23 now includes a parenthesis that voids the purpose the original compiler had in mind, namely the tracing of Jesus' lineage through Joseph. It reads: "Jesus...being the son (as was supposed) of Joseph...." Assuming that gross inconsistency may serve as a valid clue for discerning a later insertion, the genealogy was probably composed by someone who believed Jesus was actually Joseph's offspring.

If the small but significant addition to the original text of Luke 1:34 is acknowledged and rejected, then the opening chapter of the Third Gospel contains two birth stories that express the Jewish outlook on dual paternity with exquisite artistry. No other chapter of the New Testament has a more Hebraic tone; even apart from the profuse allusions to and quotations from Jewish Scriptures, many idioms are Semitic.[38] The writer of the narrative doubtlessly had the birth story of Samuel in mind when he composed what Luke incorporated into his Gospel. Some scholars offer sound linguistic reasons for maintaining that the birth stories were first written down in Hebrew or Aramaic and then translated into Greek.[39]

Luke's Gospel opens with the story of Elizabeth conceiving a child after the normal years of childbearing had passed. The story of the conception of Elizabeth's son John is markedly similar to the story of Samson's conception.[40] In both, an angel announces the coming of a child to a wife who has been infertile. It is implied, but not explicitly stated, that the husbands Zechariah and Manoah impregnated their wives. To emphasize God's role in this divine-human triangle, the writer comments after Gabriel's visitation: "Elizabeth conceived ...saying, 'Thus the Lord has done to me in the days when he looked on me, to take away my reproach among men.' " The announcements by Gabriel to Elizabeth and to Mary are parallel; the angel promises sons and says the Holy Spirit will be active during their pre-natal state.

In light of the cultural patterns of ancient Palestine, the prophecy that a betrothed young woman will conceive is not unusual. Betrothal in the Hebrew culture legally constituted a marital relationship,[41] for there was no wedding service conducted by a priest or by a state officer in the biblical era. Not long after the betrothal was arranged, the groom had the privilege of having sexual relations with his bride. Tobias, a devout Jew, cohabitated immediately following his betrothal. People would not have been surprised therefore, if his wife became pregnant before the wedding feast, which was held later.[42] The Mishnah indicates that marital consummation occasionally occurred while the betrothed girl was still residing in her parents' house.[43] The young wife could be a virgin (*bethulah*), since the term referred to "whoever has never menstruated even though she is married."[44] A *bethulah* could even be a mother who became impregnated at her first ovulation.[45]

In Judaism non-conjugal marriage was a contradiction in terms. According to the Torah it was the husband's sacred duty to give his wife her marital rights.[46] In this regard Marcus Cohn has pointed out that "the most important common obligation of the married couple is the performance of the marital act."[47] Paul introduces that Jewish custom into Christianity when he insists that sexual relations is the right and duty of all married couples.[48]

Clarity of understanding has been diminished by the translation given a crucial term in Luke's annunciation story. *Parthenos* is usually translated "virgin," an English word designating a person who has not had sexual intercourse. However, *parthenos* is best defined, in both biblical and nonbiblical usage, as a girl who has reached marriageable age.[49] In Luke 1:27 it refers to Mary who is entering sexual maturity in contrast to Elizabeth who was presumed, before she became pregnant, to have reached menopause. Due to the fact that a *parthenos* customarily married at the age of puberty and that social sanctions protected unwed Hebrew daughters from seduction, a *parthenos* would probably not be sexually experienced prior to betrothal. Even so, *parthenos* could refer to an unbethrothed girl who had engaged in coitus. In the Septuagint it is used to describe a girl who had been raped, as well as a wife.[50] Moreover, in classical Greek *parthenos* could refer to a non-virginal young woman; in a nonliterary papyrus, the word refers to a mother; and in Jewish sepulcher inscriptions during the early Christian era, it connoted someone who had married.[51] After a careful examination of the terms translated as "virgin" in ancient Jewish and Christian literature, J.M. Ford concludes: "The term 'virgin' is not necessarily confined to one who has not experienced coitus, but, on the one hand, may be used of a minor who has married and been widowed, and, on the other, of people who have only taken one spouse during their lifetime."[52]

In Luke 1:35, Gabriel informs Mary of the means by which she will conceive: "The Holy Spirit will come upon you,/ And the power of the Most High will overshadow you." This couplet of synonymous parallelism discreetly implies that God will perform a husband's role. The way the Spirit figuratively descends upon Mary is analogous to the spread-the-husband's-skirt-over idiom for coitus in Hebrew Scripture.[53] A literal intepretation of this bit of poetry about the spirit's union with Mary does violence to the Hebraic outlook. G.B. Caird perceptively comments: "It would never have occurred to a Jew to consider the overshadowing of Mary by the Holy Spirit as a substitute for normal parenthood."[54] The Hebrew religion was distinctive in the ancient world in demythologizing and thereby humanizing sexuality.[55] The Jews did not think God actually copulated with goddesses or with human women. Consequently, Luke's account of divine paternity may be a metaphor showing that God was active in bringing Jesus into the world. After the generation is symbolically accomplished by the Heavenly Father and biologically by the earthly husband, the embryo in Mary's uterus had a normal gestation period and delivery.

Since scholars generally agree that Luke edited written tradition he collected from Palestinian sources pertaining to Jesus' birth, and since the original story was patterned after stories of outstanding personages of Hebrew history who were conceived by the combined efforts of God, men, and women, was it Luke or was it some later scribe who inserted the clauses in Luke 1:34 and 3:24 that contradict the dual paternity notion?

The paucity of information about Luke makes this question difficult to answer. However, several shreds of evidence point to someone who lived after Luke as the one who converted the dual paternity story into a virginal conception story. Firstly, Luke would hardly have been so inconsistent as to state Joseph was Jesus' father in the Jerusalem temple and in the Nazareth synagogue episodes, and then express an opposing view in the genealogy placed between those episodes. If Luke believed that Jesus was not in Joseph's line of descent, why would he include the genealogy? Secondly, scholars know Luke's text was tampered with by a medieval scribe who deleted references to Joseph as Jesus' father. As a result, sentence subjects in Luke

2:33 and 2:43 read, according to the King James version (based on the altered Greek text), "Joseph and his mother." The older manuscripts show that the translation should be "his father and his mother" or "his parents." Luke 1:34 and 3:23 were probably similarly changed by other copyists who wanted to square Luke's nativity story with the beliefs of some church fathers in the efficacy of holy virgins. Thirdly, the Greek conjunction *epei*, meaning "since," is used dozens of times in the New Testament, but in the writings of Luke (which are one-third of the New Testament) *epei* only introduces the clause "since I know not a man," in Luke 1:34. In other passages Luke employs different terms to convey the same meaning, so the *epei* clause was probably inserted by someone other than Luke. Fourthly, a characteristic of Luke's theology is that the Holy Spirit works through the interaction of human agents, although the process is not explained. In Acts, for example, the Holy Spirit mysteriously operates in the Antioch congregation and consequently Paul and Barnabas are designated missionaries. In another instance, Luke describes a heated discussion at a meeting of church leaders in Jerusalem, and concludes that the final consensus was the "decision of the Holy Spirit."[56] Finally, Luke lived in the first century of the Christian era and wrote many decades before any church leader became fascinated by Jesus' presumed virginal conception. The four Gospels are alike in ascribing supernatural powers to Jesus, but they do not associate such alleged power with the way in which he entered life.

Virginal Conception Mythology

Ignatius, a bishop of Syrian Antioch in the early second century, is the first "church father" to write about Jesus' birth. To combat the docetic denial of Jesus' full humanity, Ignatius stresses that Jesus was physically like other humans from womb to tomb. In one letter he advises Christians: "Be deaf to any talk that ignores Jesus Christ, of David's lineage, of Mary; who was really born, ate and drank."[57] In another letter, Ignatius affirms dual paternity: "Our God, Jesus the Christ, was conceived by Mary in accordance with God's plan—being sprung both of the seed of David and from the Holy Spirit."[58] Sometimes Ignatius refers to mother Mary as a *parthenos*,[59] which probably means "young woman" rather than "virgin." Virginity is actually excluded from the meaning of the word when he writes of "*parthenoi* who are called widows."[60] It would have gone against Ignatius' desire to show Jesus' genuine humanity to claim that his conception was only half human and thereby unlike other mortals.

An apologist named Aristides, also of the early second century, affirms this incarnation doctrine: "God came down from heaven, and from a Hebrew *parthenos* assumed and clothed himself with flesh, and the Son of God lived in a daughter of man."[61] There is no indication that *parthenos* here refers to a woman who conceived without human sexual relations.

Justin, who lived a century after the time of Jesus, is the first Christian on record to state unambiguously that Jesus was virginally conceived. Though he was aware that some Jewish Christians thought Jesus was the child of normal union between Mary and a man, Justin declares: "Christ is not man of men, begotten in the ordinary course of humanity."[62] He claims a prophecy of Isaiah as the authority for his supernaturalism. The Greek translation of Isaiah 7:14 states "a *parthenos* shall conceive." Assuming that the text has messianic reference and that the term *parthenos* refers only to a woman who has never experienced coitus, Justin argues with his Jewish adversary Trypho that Jesus must have been virginally conceived. In response, Trypho accurately points out that such a mode of birth was contrary to Jewish messianic expectations; that Isaiah was referring to an occurrence in the immediate future; and that the terminology involved pertained to a young woman, not to a virgin.[63]

Justin's argument for a virginal conception resulted from an eisegesis of Scripture, so where did such a notion originate? This question is well answered by Trypho when he accuses Christians of adapting pagan birth stories of demigod heroes to aid in propagandizing their religion. He says: "In Greek mythology there is a story of how Perseus was born of Danae while she was a virgin when the one whom they call Zeus descended upon her in the form of a golden shower." Then Trypho chides: "You Christians ought to be ashamed to relate such things like the heathen. It would be better if you asserted that this Jesus is a human being of human parentage."[64] But Justin was far from being ashamed of the parallel, and he uses it in defense of his doctrine. He asserts: "When we declare that the Logos, who is the first offspring of God, was born without sexual intercourse...we do not report anything different from your view about those called sons of Zeus."[65] Justin thought he was strengthening the appeal of Christianity in the Gentile world by admitting that there is really nothing unique about virginally conceived man. Actually he was placing Christianity on a level with superstitions that many reasonable persons had discarded.

Similar to other postapostolic church leaders, Justin had a strong Hellenistic background and correspondingly little understanding of the Hebraic outlook. He studied under some Greek philosophers and adopted their moral dualism. By associating the satanic serpent with coitus, he assumes that Jesus would have been defiled by conception through a sensual union.[66] Had Justin comprehended the Hebraic concept of dual paternity he would not have glibly presupposed that physical passion and spiritual power cannot coexist in a person.

Tertullian, writing around A.D. 200, follows Justin's line of defense by establishing a tie with Hellenistic legends of miraculous conceptions. The manner of Jesus' birth is described by the prominent Latin church father in this way: "The Son of God has a mother touched by no impurity.... When a ray is projected from the sun, it is a portion of the whole.... This ray of God...entered into a certain virgin, and, in her womb fashioned into flesh, is born, man mingled with God."[67] Tertullian acknowledges that his treatment of Jesus' virginal conception is similar to pagan stories of unnatural liaisons. The parallel he may have had in mind is the myth of sun god Apollo siring Alexander the Great. A divine ray penetrated his mother which caused her pregnancy, rather than intercourse with Philip. Plutarch tells of the conception: "The night before the marriage was consummated, the bride dreamed that there was a clap of thunder, that a bolt fell upon her womb, and that from the stroke a great fire was kindled, which broke into flames that went out in all directions and then was extinguished."[68] Tertullian makes this strange deduction about the presumed celibacy of Jesus: "Christ was himself a virgin in the flesh, in that he was born of a virgin's flesh."[69] The alleged virginity of Mary becomes for Tertullian the supreme model for women of the church, and the virginity of Jesus serves the same function for men. The belief that Jesus was a life-long virgin probably originated about the time of Tertullian, as I demonstrate in *Was Jesus Married?*[70]

In the folklore of the ancient Mediterranean world many stories attributed divine paternity, without human male procreators, to teachers and kings.[71] Such wonder tales were told of Pythagoras,[72] Plato,[73] Augustus,[74] and Apollonius.[75] Also, superman Hercules was begotten by the visitation of the Greek father-god with Alcmene. "Hail to the couch where the spousals divine with the mortal were blended," Euripides rhapsodizes: "where for love of the lady of Pereus' line, Zeus' glory descended!"[6]

Some Christians were aware of a legend that originated before the Christian era regarding the supernatural birth of

Buddha. A divine power, symbolized by the tusks of a white elephant, impregnated Queen Maya, a woman who was void of sexual desire. By a kind of miraculous Caesarean section, Buddha was later born from the same side where the tusks entered at conception.[77] Jerome charges that the pagans should not claim that Christians invented the story of virginal conception because "the founder of Buddhism had his birth through the side of a virgin."[78]

Irenaeus, the Bishop of Lyons, was the most formidable defender of the faith in the late second century and did much to entrench the dogma of the asexual conception of Jesus. Accepting Paul's doctrine that Jesus is "the last Adam," the Bishop attempts to establish an analogy between the way both were directly formed by God out of an untilled substance. By a play on the word "virgin," Irenaeus draws this parallel: "While it was still virgin, God took dust of the earth and fashioned the man, the beginning of humanity. So the Lord, summing up afresh this man, reproduced the scheme of Adam's incarnations, being born of a virgin by the will and the wisdom of God."[79] Looking at the parallel from another angle, Irenaeus reasons: "If the first Adam had had a man for his father and had been begotten by 'natural' seed, then it could rightly be asserted of the second Adam that he had been begotten by Joseph."[80]

In the latter half of the second century, when the canon of the New Testament was becoming established, it is probable that some scribes of Gentile Christianity modified the Lukan and Matthean accounts in order to give Jesus as spectacular a beginning as that of prominent figures in the ancient world. Those involved in that pious fraud no doubt believed they were doing a service to Christianity by removing holy Jesus from defilement they thought would ensue had Jesus been generated on a bed soiled by erotic passion. Around A.D. 200 a Christian gave this explanation: "Our Lord Jesus Christ was born of a virgin only for the following reason: he was to bring to naught the begetting that proceeds from lawless appetite, and show the ruler of this world that God could form man even without human sexual intercourse."[81] Here is stated the anti-Hebraic outlook that sexual desire and its fulfillment is contrary to the law of God and that those who are immaculately pure must renounce it completely.

With respect to the church's distortion of the Hebraic view of sexuality expressed in the opening story of Luke's Gospel, Thomas Walker's judgment has much to commend it. In his book *Is Not This the Son of Joseph?*, he writes:

> The original beauty of the early document, which was here utilized by the evangelist, has been spoiled by someone, whose mind was as far removed as possible from the mind of the composer of the document.... The Virgin Birth idea was an error of the Greek-minded leaders of the early Church in the second century, who...never really got entirely free from the erroneous notion of their upbringing, that the human body was the seat of evil.... They lamentably misinterpreted a Semitic story of the conception of a child of Hebrew parents.[82]

The notion of dual paternity for Jesus was lost after Christianity jelled in the second century, and the idea of Jesus' virginal conception became a part of the basic dogma. The last trace of dual paternity for Jesus in Christian literature is found in the *Gospel of Philip* which was discovered in Egypt in 1945. The authors of that apocryphal gospel, which may date back to the earliest centuries of the church, assert that they were "Hebrews prior to becoming Christians."[83] They present the traditional Hebraic outlook in declaring that Jesus was both the offspring of Joseph the carpenter and the child of the Heavenly Father who "united with the virgin."[84] They reason: "The Lord would not have said 'My Father in heaven' unless he had another father; he would have simply said 'My Father.' "[85]

The pillars of orthodoxy in the patristic era twisted the

earliest Christian testimony, claiming that Jesus was discontinuous with humanity because his mother's womb was not fertilized by the sperm of a male. By treating Mary's conception as an unnatural occurrence they magnified out of proportion the significance of the nativity in the life of Jesus and in the life of nascent Christianity. In the New Testament the circumstances of Jesus' birth are peripheral: no comment by Jesus or by his apostles is recorded about a miraculous conception, and the earliest Gospel does not even mention Jesus' birth. Yet in the creeds of the church the mode of Jesus' birth usually has as significant a place as his sufferings and resurrection. That most important fourth-century Nicene Creed implies that there is nothing worth affirming about Jesus' earthly life except his virginal birth and his manner of death. In the New Testament the uniqueness of Jesus is bound up with his way of life, which incarnated love, justice, and freedom; but in orthodoxy there has been emphasis upon his being born in a manner that was removed from the so-called tainted sensual pleasures and the corrupted sperm of Adam. The eminent theologian Anthanasius articulates the settled outlook of the fourth-century church when he states that the Logos took a human body "directly from a spotless, stainless virgin, without the agency of human father—a pure body, untainted by intercourse with man."[86] In all major branches of Eastern Orthodoxy and Latin Catholicism the Athanasian position has been declared to be true. That position is also widely accepted in Protestantism even to the present time. Reformed theologian Karl Barth, for example, asserts:

> The sinful life of sex is excluded as the source of the human existence of Jesus Christ.... The event of sex cannot be considered at all as the sign of the divine *agape* which seeks not its own and never fails.... If Christ were the son of a male He would be a sinner like all the rest.[87]

The later church fathers were not content with the dogma that Jesus was virginally conceived. Believing with Jerome that *omnis coitus impurus,*[88] they rejected earlier assumptions that Mary was no longer an intact virgin after being pregnant with Jesus. They refused to accept the New Testament claim that Joseph had carnal knowledge of Mary after Jesus was born.[89] Although Tertullian had an exalted view of the status of virgins, he argues against the growing belief in Mary's perpetual virginity. He claims that she was "virgin in terms of a husband, not virgin in terms of giving birth."[90] Also that Latin father believes that the brothers and sisters of Jesus referred to in the Gospels were procreated by Joseph and Mary.[91] Some church leaders, however, drew on an apocryphal story written in the second century to justify their belief that Mary's hymen never ruptured. An influential tract entitled *The Protevangelium of James* maintains that Jesus' brothers are step-brothers from the first marriage of Joseph, and that he was an impotent widower when he married Mary. Moreover, to show that Mary was not only a virgin after the birth of Jesus but was *virgo intacto* during her delivery, a conversation between Mary's midwife and Salome is recorded. When the latter is informed that Mary did not lose her virginity when Jesus was born, Salome confirms the truth of the midwife's report by personally investigating.[92]

Jerome is offended by the nerve of Helvidius, a scholarly contemporary, who contended that marital sexuality was as holy as virginal abstinence and cited as proof holy Mary, who became pregnant several times after intercourse. Helvidius points out that Jesus is called Mary's "first-born" (*prototokos*), although Luke uses another term (*monogenes*) to refer to a person who procreates only one child.[93] But Jerome not only believes that the mother of Jesus did not engage in sex after her singular giving of birth, but that her hymen was not broken during that parturition. Presuming that a verse in the Song of

Songs was a prophecy of Mary's life-long condition, Jerome announces a miraculous delivery that enabled her to remain "a fountain sealed."[94] Jerome's innovative mind associates the passing of Jesus through a closed vagina with his passing through a closed door after his resurrection.[95] He believes both movements were supernatural. Augustine also believes that Mary was "a virgin before, during, and after Jesus' birth" and drew on canonical Scripture for support. He allegorizes a verse from Ezekiel: "This gate shall remain shut, it shall not be opened, and no man shall pass through it; because the Lord God of Israel has entered by it."[96] In this description of the restored Jerusalem temple, Augustine finds reference to Joseph not trespassing across his wife's closed vagina.

Centuries later Aquinas, the pre-eminent theologian of Roman Catholicism, accepts the position of Jerome and Augustine on Mary's virginity, and shares Jerome's anger toward Helvidius' sensible position. Aquinas writes:

> Without any hesitation we must abhor the error of Helvidius, who dared to assert that Christ's mother, after his birth, was carnally known by Joseph, and bore other children.... This error is an insult to the Holy Spirit, whose shrine was the virginal womb, wherein he had formed the flesh of Christ. Thus it was unbecoming that it should be desecrated by intercourse with man.[97]

Aquinas audaciously affirms that there was no "unlocking of the enclosure of virginal purity,"[98] in spite of the reference in Luke to Jesus "opening the womb." Even though Jesus came forth through the vagina, "the Blessed Virgin gave birth to her Son by a miracle."[99] Thus Aquinas, who articulates the most rational expression of medieval Christianity, sets firmly in place another layer of supernaturalist doctrine pertaining to the birth of Jesus.

Aquinas borrows Greek biological theory in order to

explain how virginal conception delivered Jesus from original sin.[100] From the Latin fathers onward it has been a basic dogma in European Christianity that the fallen nature of the first human couple has been congenitally transmitted.[101] The Greeks believed the sperm alone conveyed the non-material intelligible form of humanness to offspring and that woman merely provided the moist matter and receptacle for incubating the seed. A drama of Aeschylus, for example, contains these lines: "The so-called offspring is not produced by the mother. She is no more than the nurse, as it were, of the newly conceived fetus. It is the male who is the author of its being."[102] Hence, a virginally conceived Jesus could not inherit sin, according to Aquinas, for a mother could not transmit character qualities to her child.

Ever since ovulation was discovered in 1827 scientists have recognized both male and female contribute equally to the genetic characteristics of their offspring. In a frantic attempt to restore Catholic confidence in a bankrupt doctrine, Pope Pius IX announced the Dogma of the Immaculate Conception of Mary in 1854. The "infallible" declaration is interpreted to mean that all taint of original sin was miraculously removed from Mary at the moment of her conception, that she was liberated from sexual desire, and that she was made incapable of sinning.[103] Being more pure than angels, this unique woman could not infect the fruit of her womb, even though all other mothers and fathers transmit sinfulness to their children. Pius attempted to rewrite history by stating that his dogma "always existed in the church." Ironically, what is now a mandatory belief in Roman Catholicism was rejected as unsound by Aquinas, the most influential medieval contributor to the adoration of Mary. [104] Attempting to build the idea of Jesus' perfection on genetic foundations is a blunder.

Henry Morris, a leading polemicist for American fundamentalism, uses another dodge in an attempt to resolve the dilemma precipitated by modern genetics. To prevent the transmission of a sinful nature into Jesus, he claims the zygote nurtured in Mary's womb was "formed neither of the seed of the man nor the egg of the woman."[105] To protect Jesus from the alleged corruption of fallen mankind that would have been conveyed by the chromosomes of either male or female parent, Moore presumes that God directly created *ex nihilo* the perfect zygote for the second Adam, even as he had done for the first Adam. Like the mysterious priest-king Melchizedek referred to in Hebrews 7:3, Jesus "is without father or mother or genealogy." Even though he lacked real human parents, Mary became the surrogate matrix for the divine implantation.

Biological and Theological Difficulties

The apostles held that Jesus was without sin because of his godly decisions and actions throughout his ministry. Judging from Acts and the letters of the New Testament, Paul and the other early missionaries never mentioned virginal conception, and accordingly it is not in the confessional statements of the earliest church. Those who insist that the alleged "virgin birth of Christ" is central to Christianity err both in evaluating it as factual history and in declaring it essential theology. Gordon Kaufman rightly views the virgin birth doctrine as a threat to the foundational Christian claim that God became human. That Harvard theologian comments on the doctrine:

> It does not portray Jesus as either truly God or truly man: he is apparently half and half. A kind of pasted-together being, he not unreasonably is taken by many moderns to be simply a piece of fantastic and incredible mythology, rather than the one point within human history which is a genuine clue to ultimate reality, the very *man* who is the revelation of the very *God*.[106]

Paul Tillich also uses orthodoxy in criticism of orthodoxy: he rejects the doctrine of the virgin birth because it "takes away one of the fundamental doctrines of Chalcedon," namely that of the full humanity of Christ.[107] Dietrich Bonhoeffer makes the same point in the incisive query: "Does it not miss the decisive point of the incarnation by implying that Jesus has *not* become man wholly as we are?"[108]

The doctrine of virginal conception could more accurately be called the doctrine of virginal deception, for it falsifies the core of Christian belief. The earliest Christians had little difficulty in believing that Jesus was both the son of Joseph and the Son of God, but later theologians, who did not appreciate the dual paternity paradox, engaged in historical fabrications to eliminate Joseph from the paternity triangle. Jerome even went so far as to declare that Joseph was a life-long virgin.[109]

To make the alleged virginal conception of Jesus more palatable to reasonable Christians, there have been furtive attempts in the course of church history to interpret it in a non-supernatural manner. Origen points out that parthenogenesis is a scientific fact for some animal species. That early Christian apologist argued that God has created vultures who can reproduce asexually, so it is not incredible for such to be done by a human.[110] In contemporary zoology there is additional evidence of eggs developing independently of fertilization. Bees, frogs, and turkeys have been stimulated to reproduce without sperm fertilization. Only female clones appear to be a genetic possibility in virginal conceptions. Even though parthenogenesis is a natural though rare occurrence for some animals less complex than mammals, how is this relevant to the doctrine of Jesus' virginal conception? Do not those who advocate it want to show that Jesus' conception is unique and unlike that of any other creature?

Scientific objections to the Gospel nativity stories can be reduced if the biblical view of dual paternity is used in their interpretation. Ancient though it is, the dual paternity theory joins modern biology in rejecting human conception without insemination. The revival of that theory would result in a fuller recognition that divine activity does not exclude human cooperation. This should be corrective to the supernaturalists who find the divine mainly in the events in which "sense is numb and flesh retires." Those who can find nothing spiritual in carnal intercourse need to recall that the first blessing in the Bible is on marital sexuality. The frowning disapproval of sexual passion in the history of Western civilization has in no little way been influenced by those who have wrongly given an asexual interpretation to the relationship between Mary and Joseph, and then have exalted them as models of holiness.[111]

Conversely, the naturalist should see in a theory of dual paternity that human endeavors do not exclude the divine presence. The God of the Bible is found more in the warp and woof of ordinary human intercourse than inexplicable extraordinary events. Human sexuality can be not only a means of hedonistic gratification but also an area where God's love and mercy is discerned. The dual paternity theory provides a middle ground that is more theologically adequate, more scientifically plausible, and more historically sound than the polar positions that have all too often been evoked by a consideration of Jesus' nativity. Those who champion the theory see the conception of Jesus not as a case of *either* the Spirit giving life to Mary's ovum *or* Joseph's sperm fertilizing it. Rather Jesus was *both* the pure enfleshment of God *and* the complete human that was formed by the union of male and female genes.

J.A.T. Robinson notes that the purpose of the story of Mary conceiving Jesus with divine assistance was to make a positive claim about the Spirit, not a negative assertion about the flesh. He interprets the story as being on as different a level from the science of genetics as Genesis is from geology. It is saying, he claims, "that the significance of Jesus is not to be comprehended *simply* at the level of heredity and environment."[112]

The literary-historical investigation of Jesus' generation can be compared with the scientific treatments of man's genesis.

Until organic evolution was defended by Charles Darwin and others, a consensus judgment in Western civilization was that the birth of mankind came about a few thousand years ago with the creation of Adam and his spouse by God's special intervention. Then came the theory of natural selection, which was heatedly debated by Europeans in the nineteenth century and by Americans in the twentieth. Out of this debate most of the scholarly Christians and Jews came to realize that Darwin's theory of natural selection was compatible with the doctrine that God created the universe. Indeed, the origin of humanity as a distinct species by descent from some lower form is regarded by Darwin himself as a beautiful expression of the Creator's order. Darwin, whose academic training was mainly in theology, touches on this in the conclusions of his two major works. In rejecting the mythology that God directly functions as a bio-chemical agent, he writes: "To my mind it accords better with what we know of the laws impressed on matter by the Creator, that the production and extinction of the past and present inhabitants of the world should have been due to secondary causes." Drawing on philosophical theology, Darwin here acknowledges God as the primary cause of life but dignifies secondary or scientific causation as the way in which God works in the world. Darwin finds "grandeur" in the view that the Creator acts best through biological regularity rather than in the alleged abrogations of nature's order.[113]

Many view Darwin as doing a service to religion by freeing the opening chapters of Genesis from a literalistic interpretation. They think of the Creator not as one who during six days said a few momentous words that formed all the present species but as an immanent Spirit who is perennially creative through the chemical elements of nature. A dual causality is operative: God is understood as the ultimate cause of the universe and the distinctive spirit of man, but evolutionary process is recognized as the method by which all life is created.

Vast numbers of conservatives and fundamentalists in

Christianity, Judaism, and Islam still do not believe human evolution to be true. The most comprehensive study ever made of a religious group in the United States reveals that 70 percent of Lutherans agree, at least in part, with the statement, "The belief that human beings descended from some low animal form is contrary to the Word of God and un-Christian."[114] When George Gallup asked a sample of the general American public to select the statement that came closest to describing their belief about human origins, most chose a theological response, and one that rejected organic evolution. The survey, taken a few years ago, shows that the most basic assumption in biological science has not been integrated into the world-view of a large majority of Americans, inasmuch as 50 percent prefer the statement "God created Adam and Eve, which was the start of human life," while 31 percent prefer the statement that "God began an evolutionary cycle for all living things." Presumably the Adam and Eve story will continue to be interpreted in a more literal than liberal manner, for 70 percent of the clergy under 30 years of age take that stance compared to 57 percent of the clergy over 50.[115]

The reconciliation between science and religion faces similar problems with respect to the birth of the one whom Paul calls the "Second Adam." The traditional theory of Jesus' conception was first discussed intensely by European scholars in the nineteenth century. Then, in a movement paralleling in time and place the debate over biological evolution, shock waves of the Christological argument reached America in the first part of the twentieth century. During the past generation the discussion, coupled with heresy trials, has subsided, but unfortunately this is not due to Christians having arrived at a general consensus on the issue. Memories of harsh fundamentalism-modernism fights and a proneness to let a sleeping dogma lie are more operative in this diminishing of debate than is general agreement. On the basis of a 1964 sociological survey, four-fifths of the Roman Catholics and over half of the Protestants accept as completely true the statement, "Jesus was born of a virgin."[116] A 1972 study of the major branches of American Lutheranism discloses that belief in the virgin birth of Jesus is the most firmly held belief of the denomination. Only 8 percent agreed with this statement of dual paternity: "Jesus is the supreme revelation of God to men, but he was conceived like anyone else. In a sense any child is divinely conceived."[117]

A *rapprochement* might be accomplished between the supernaturalist and the naturalist points of view if both sides could accept the idea which Paul received from his Hebrew heritage, that the dynamic Spirit of God need not circumvent the natural processes in generating nature in its totality, or in generating Jesus in particular. An adaptation of Darwin's postscript to his *Descent of Man* is in order:

> I am aware that the conclusions arrived at in this work will be denounced by some as highly irreligious; but he who denounces them is bound to show why it is more irreligious to explain the conception of Jesus through the laws of ordinary reproduction. The birth of individuals and species are equally part of that grand sequence of events that our minds refuse to accept as the result of blind chance.

3

THE GROWTH OF A
MATERIALIZED RESURRECTION

During the first century of Christianity there was a major shift in viewpoint on the nature of the life after death. Initially it was believed that God resurrected Jesus spiritually and that such would be the pattern for other righteous humans. Within a few years, however, the earliest position became transposed into a doctrine of fleshly resurrection for both bad and good people. That heightened supernaturalism has been accepted as basic truth by most Christians across the centuries. There was a progressive materialization of the resurrection doctrine and in some ways pivotal leaders of Catholicism and Protestantism have been of one mind on the subject.

Paul's Resurrection Views

1 Corinthians 15 contains both the earliest documentation of the resurrection of Jesus and a discussion of its implications for Christians. What Paul records there and in his other letters is at least a decade older than resurrection accounts found elsewhere in the New Testament. While chronological priority in recording does not in itself prove that an account is more reliable, the likelihood that such is the case increases if its writer is reputed to be at least as honest as the later writers. In response to doubts expressed by some Corinthian Christians about the paradoxical claim that dead persons might continue to live, Paul sets down the oral tradition of Jesus' tragedy and triumph conveyed to him, probably within five years of the crucifixion. The apostle testifies:

> I passed on to you, as of first importance, what I received: that Christ died for our sins as the Scriptures foretold; that he was buried, and that he was raised three days later, as the Scriptures foretold; and that he appeared to Cephas and then to the Twelve. After that, he appeared to more than five hundred brothers simultaneously, most of whom are still alive, though some have gone to their rest. Then he appeared to James and afterward to all the apostles. Last of all, as to one untimely born, he appeared to me.

Trying to muster the strongest proof possible, the apostle presents in historical order the names of those individuals and groups who witnessed the resurrected Jesus. One of the groups is composed of the apostles and the other contains hundreds of Christians. He refers to Peter and James, church leaders who would have been well known, and concludes his list by affirming his own experience as being of equivalent quality to that of Peter and the others, because he uses identical language in referring to it. Also, in other letters he singles out the experience of seeing the resurrected Christ as the prime prerequisite for the office of apostleship.[1]

An invaluable help for analyzing the various New Testament accounts of Jesus' resurrection is provided by Paul's assumption that the risen Christ "appeared" to other individuals in a way similar to the apostle's own inaugural revelation. In Paul's letters there is a considerable amount of first-hand testimony about his initiating Christian experience, and it does not contain legendary material that usually arises from oral transmission. The best avenue for understanding the Easter experiences of the earliest Christians is to presume they were like Paul's "Damascus Road experience." By relying on information written down *by* the person experiencing what is being described, we can establish a basis on which to judge the historicity of second-hand resurrection accounts *about* the apostles recorded years later in the New Testament.

Significantly, even an eminent Synoptic Gospels specialist has recognized that it is to the letters of Paul that one must go for clarity on Jesus' resurrection. In *The Resurrection According to Matthew, Mark, and Luke*, the last book Norman Perrin wrote before his death, this crucial perspective is provided:

> The Christian who asks the modern question, what actually happened on that first Easter morning? must come to terms with the Apostle Paul. Paul is the one witness we have whom we can interrogate about his claim to have seen Jesus as risen, and our assumption has to be that if we could interrogate the other witnesses their claims would be similiar to his. In some way they were granted a vision of Jesus which convinced them that God had vindicated Jesus out of his death.[2]

To understand adequately what Paul meant by his declaration that Christ "appeared" to him, it is necessary to draw on descriptions he provides of his religious state before and after this Christophany. Paul's autobiographical comments in two letters are brief but telling. He is proud to have been born into a Jewish family, for this distinguished him from the proselyte who became aware of Judaism only as an adult. He writes of his zealous adherence to the standards of his religion and of his awareness of having surpassed many fellow Jews in devotion to ancient tradition.[3] Before his conversion, his prayers might well have resembled this one from the Talmud: "I thank you, O Lord my God, that you have set my lot with those who sit in the house of learning, and not with those who sit at the street corners. I and they rise early—I to the words of the Law, but they to things of no account."[4] Paul belonged to the sect of Pharisees which, as Josephus points out, "valued highly the exact skill they had in the law of their fathers, and made men believe they were highly favored by God."[5] Accordingly, the apostle states that he was "faultlessly righteous" in abiding by the law of Moses.[6]

What did Paul know of Jesus before his Christophany? At a minimum he was aware that Jesus was crucified while leading a band of Jews who viewed him as the fulfillment of their Scripture's promise of a Messianic ruler. In the pre-conversion period of his life, Paul thought it blasphemy to associate God's specially anointed one with anyone who had been crucified. This was absolutely prohibited by the Law, for it declares: "Cursed be everyone who hangs on a tree."[7] The Pentateuch text gave the young fanatic sufficient justification for launching a campaign to exterminate Christians.

While he was trying to destroy the church in the Damascus area, Paul testifies, he had a religious experience like a prophet of Israel.[8] Jeremiah spoke of his initial vision as containing this word from the Lord: "Before you were born I selected you to be a prophet to the nations."[9] Likewise Paul affirms: "He who selected me before I was born, and called me through his grace, chose to reveal his Son in me in order that I might proclaim him to the nations." Further on in the Galatian letter, from which this testimony comes, Paul clarifies that this revelation was not an external phenomenon, as portrayed in secondary sources. Using the same preposition, *ev*, basically meaning *within*, he states this paradox: "I live no more but Christ lives in me."[10] Paul states there that he "died" to the demands of the Law so that he might "live" for God. He thinks of that symbolic death as a reenactment of Jesus' crucifixion. In an existential manner, Paul is a participant in Jesus' death and resurrection, not a spectator to it. He views himself more as one who lives *in* Christ than as one who lives *after* him. Jesus is a present reality to Paul and by means of an ego-reorientation, the central values of his "Lord" are internalized.

Paralleling the autobiographical sketch in Galatians, Paul looks back in Philippians to his previous confidence in a life of legal rectitude and evaluates it as garbage—or something stronger than garbage. He then writes of "sharing Christ's suffering and of concomitantly experiencing "the power of his resurrection."[11] Finding that mystical bond a pearl of superlative value, he willingly gave up his prestigious status in Judaism in exchange for it.

Paul's new way of living resulted in large part from a fresh interpretation of his Jewish Bible. He now sees that a suffering Messiah is in accord with passages that he had overlooked in earlier study. He can now endorse the judgment transmitted to him by the earliest Christians, "that Christ died for our sins as the Scriptures foretold." Judging by scriptural quotations made elsewhere in the New Testament, the account in Isaiah 53 of a suffering servant who eventually became triumphant, is the main passage on which the church based its authority. At some point in Paul's activities as a persecutor of Christianity, he came to understand that God's agent of reconciliation would achieve victory through apparent failure, and that Jesus' mission thus confirmed the deepest strata of prophetic Scriptures.

The apostle assumes that his intimate conversion experience

was not unlike that which all Christians experience. Using plural pronouns, he maintains that "our old self was crucified with him" and tells of its consequences: "If we have been united with him in a death like his, we shall certainly be united with him in a resurrection like his."[12] He requests members of the Corinthian congregation to test the genuineness of their faith by asking themselves, "Is Jesus Christ within?"[13] Therefore, the focal point of Pauline Christianity is a corporate fellowship of those who have become "a new creation"[14] after undergoing an intensely personal identification with the crucified and resurrected Christ. A new ethic accompanies this re-creation: "If then you have been raised with Christ, seek the things that are above:...compassion, kindness, humility, gentleness, patience,...forgiveness,...and love."[15]

In one passage Paul compares the experience of becoming a Christian to that of inward enlightenment. God who created light, he affirms, "shone in our hearts to bring us the light of knowledge—God's glory in the face of Christ."[16] This experience of brightness is similar to the radiant revelation to two Israelite prophets. Moses' burning bush theophany at Mount Sinai is described in this way: "The angel of the Lord appeared (ophthe, Septuagint) to him in a flame of fire out of the midst of a bush."[17] It is significant that the same verb is used here that Paul uses in describing the appearance of the risen Christ. The Deuteronomic theologian was insistent in pointing out that "no form" of God was seen when fire accompanied divine revelations at the holy mountain.[18] Isaiah also had an initiating religious experience that was associated with a glorious vision that included fire. After he "saw the Lord" as exalted but still intimately in the temple, he was cleansed by a glowing coal from the altar of burnt offering. That vision of a thrice holy God gave the prophet insight into individual and corporate sin and inspired him to go forth and face suffering.[19]

The momentous vision of Blaise Pascal has overtones of the personal revelations that Moses, Isaiah, and Paul received.

The phrases the Frenchman later jotted down indicate that he had an entrancing sensation of fire. This brought him to a vivid awareness of his separation from the "God of Abraham, God of Isaac, God of Jacob" and the "God of Jesus Christ." He confesses: "I have fled from him, denied him, crucified him."[20] Out of this came an experience of joyful unity. Pascal's subsequent life was radically changed by that transcending experience.

In analyzing Paul's own record of his conversion we find no evidence that he was confronted with experiences from objects that could have been recorded on audio-visual equipment, had such been invented and present. Paul, in contrast to the account of Acts 9, wrote of no heavenly voices heard by him and his Damascus road companions—of no miraculous loss of sight and later restoration as a scale-like substance fell from his eyes. However, he does not regard his encounter with Christ as a fantasy he had projected. On the contrary, he treats his initiating vision as the most real and motivating event of his life.

Tillich regards Christ's resurrection as central to Christian theology, but calls it an "absurdity" and "blasphemy" to interpret it as a corpse revival account. He expresses his "restitution theory" in this way:

> The concrete individual life of the man Jesus of Nazareth is raised above transitoriness into the eternal presence of God as Spirit. This event happened first to some of his followers who had fled to Galilee in the hours of his execution; then to many others; then to Paul; then to all those who in every period experience his living presence here and now.... The preceding theory...places at the center of its analysis the religious meaning of the Resurrection for the disciples (and all their followers), in contrast to their previous state of negativity and despair. This view is the ecstatic confirmation of the indestructible unity of the New Being and its bearer, Jesus of Nazareth.... The Resurrection is the restitution of Jesus as the Christ, a restitution

which is rooted in the personal unity between Jesus and God and in the impact of this unity on the minds of the apostles.[21]

Tillich is rightly convinced that his interpretation is faithful to what Paul writes about the resurrection experience.

Plato is of help in explaining the complexity of religious experience. "The psychic eye," he suggests, is better for seeing the divine than ten thousand visual perceptions, "for by it alone is truth beheld."[22] What Moses, Isaiah, Paul, and Pascal saw came from behind, not before, their eyeballs. If their optic nerves were triggered, that resulted from what was internal and psychological, not from what was external and physiological. God is not a thing but a subject, so revelation happens within the minds of personal subjects. When Paul asserts: "Have I not seen Jesus?"[23] he, like Isaiah in the temple, is referring more to *in*sight and conception than to *eye*sight and perception. Since the transcending God is acknowledged by these mystics to be the primary stimulus for their experiences, it would be inadequate to refer to them as self-induced hallucinations.

In order to convince his readers that they should reject the "naive supernaturalist" interpretation of mystical experiences, Rudolf Otto relates the visions of Isaiah and Paul in this manner:

Has God a body? Is He really seated upon a throne, or has He any place in a physical sense? Do beings such as the Cherubim and Seraphim...surround Him in visible form? Has He a voice audible to our actual sense of hearing?...And if we pass on to the Resurrection-experience of Paul on the road to Damascus, do we not at once recognize the same characteristic features? Have we here sense-perception or spiritual experience? Paul nowhere describes how and in what form he beheld the Risen Christ. That does not in itself make it the less likely that he did see Him in some form, probably as a royal figure or radiant glory rather than merely as a dazzling light. The material of his vision was no doubt supplied him by the current ideas of his time concerning royal splendour and messianic kinghood, and then his faculty of vision gave this material an individual and special form. That is but to say that the vision would have a vesture of outward form just as that of Isaiah did; but this does not, for Paul any more than for Isaiah, touch the inmost import of the experience, which is here: "*He lives*; He lives as the accepted of God, the preserved of God, the exalted of God, the transfigured of God, as the conqueror of Judgment, of the Cross, and of Death."[24]

There is another fruitful approach for understanding what Paul meant when he claims that the post-mortem Christ "appeared" to many Christians. He encourages readers of his letters to think about the resurrection of dead people generally and draw parallels between how that happens and the quality of Christ's resurrection. Paul is convinced that the general human resurrection and the specific resurrection of Christ share the same nature:

> If the dead are not raised, then Christ has not been raised.... But the truth is that Christ has been raised from death.... As we have worn the likeness of the man made of dust, so we shall wear the likeness of the heavenly man.... Christ will change our humble body and make it conform to his glorious body.[25]

The apostle thinks of Christians' resurrected bodies as having been refashioned so that they are like a bright substance. In 1 Corinthians 15, he compares resurrected individuals to the variety of splendor coming from different stars. However, the metaphor falls short in that stars are radiating natural bodies whereas Paul claims there is nothing physical in the resurrected body. To reinforce his conviction that every resurrected body is exclusively a spirit body, he states emphatically: "This I say, brothers, that flesh and blood can never possess the kingdom of God and the perishable cannot possess immortality."[26] Paul does not believe that "dem bones gonna rise ag'in." He frankly and plainly declares it is not the case that the buried corpse will be raised. He does not believe that tomb dust or urn ash will be the substance of a new heavenly organism. In reference to eating, Paul states that the stomach will be destroyed by death:[27] by extrapolation, all organs of the body will perish. The transformation of a person to the immortal life is for Paul separable from physique-reconstruction. There is no evidence that he thinks of either Christ, "the first fruit,"[28] or the full crop of resurrected Christians as returning to the conditions of earthly life. The dead Christian is "away from the body and at home with the Lord."[29] Since the Host of that heavenly home is non-physical, it is fitting that God's companions should be reconstituted of a spiritual substance.

In his recent article entitled "St. Paul and the Decline of the Miraculous," Thomas Best comments on the absence of the supernatural in Paul's treatment of the resurrection:

> In contrast to the modern tendency to think of the resurrection as the "biggest" miracle, Paul does not understand it in the conventional category as "miraculous." That is, it is not for him a unique event creating a radical disjunction in history and violating the laws of nature.... While Jesus was the first to have experienced such a resurrection, he was not unique but prototypical, the "first fruits" to be followed by all believers, who in the meantime are experiencing the Spirit as the "down payment" on their later resurrection (2 Cor. 5:5).[30]

Willi Marxsen, a renowned contemporary New Testament scholar, has examined thoroughly what the early Christians meant by resurrection. He states:

> When Paul speaks of the earthly body (it would be better to translate it as the earthly "I"), this earthly "I" can be seen and touched and can eat and drink; it is "flesh and blood." The risen "I" (that is, the spiritual body) exists in a form which is completely separated from this mode of existence.[31]

According to Paul, immortality is a quality that some "put on" at death.[32] He does not share the characteristic Greek belief that souls are naturally immortal. Humans are, however, immor*table*; that is, each has a deathless potentiality that becomes actual by responding to God's gift. The apostle expresses his doctrine of conditional immortality in this way: "To those who keep on doing good and aim at glory, honor, and immortality, God will give eternal life."[33] The eternal or timeless life is therefore not an inherent right but a privilege extended to all whom God finds acceptable.

Paul balances his positive hope with a negative forecast: "The wages of sin is death, but the gift of God is eternal life through union with Christ Jesus our Lord."[34] Paul never writes that God resurrects the wicked and sends them to some infernal hell for punishment. Rather, "their end is destruction, for their god is their appetites, their glory is what they should be ashamed of, and their minds are absorbed in earthly things."[35] The apostle believes each person has the option of passing out of existence or of "passing on." The result of not being united with God is self-destruction, not an everlasting life in a place of horrible physical and mental suffering. Those who are not concerned to become infused with the immortal Spirit of God, and accept the resulting responsibilities, have nothing within them that can survive biological death. Eschatology authority R.H. Charles writes: "There could be no resurrection of the wicked according to St. Paul.... To share in the resurrection...is the privilege only of those who are spiritually one with Christ and quickened by the Holy Spirit."[36] Charles points out that an opposite view is advanced in other parts of the New Testament. For example, the Gospel of John represents Jesus as prophesying: "The time is coming when all who are in the tombs will hear the Son of God's voice and come forth: those who have done good, to the resurrection of life, and those who have done evil, to the resurrection of judgment."[37]

Other New Testament Views

Having examined Paul's resurrection doctrine, we have the perspective needed to reflect on how he might have interpreted the Easter experience of Simon Peter. In this regard Luke and Paul have one basic agreement, that Peter was the one to whom Christ first appeared. "The Lord is risen indeed," the apostles exclaim, "and has appeared to Simon!"[38] Presuming that Peter's encounter was essentially similar to his own, Paul accepts those stories being circulated which suggest that Peter's outlook shifted radically within a few days of Jesus' crucifixion. Due to cultural conditioning, Peter had earlier associated success, not rejection, with God's Messiah. Thus he had a mental block against accepting Jesus' teaching that he would be killed as a common criminal. However, the crucifixion was for Peter a kind of shock treatment. Although bewildered, he turns over in his mind memories of Jesus' life and thinks about some fresh interpretations of Scripture that Jesus had given. Peter attempts to reconcile them with those Messianic prophecies of a militant king who would be like David. In searching the Scripture, he found in Isaiah 53 and Psalm 22 intimations of a man approved by God who had suffered and died. After mulling over the matter for several days and talking with other despairing disciples, Peter suddenly intuits that defeat is a part of the Messiah's mission and that it fulfills some of the expectations of Israelite prophets. It dawns upon him that Jesus expressed dramatically God's holy love during his last days in Jerusalem and that his teacher's transforming spirit is still with him. Peter's insight is contagious, for other companions of Jesus came to understand that they had been looking for the ultimate disclosure of God in the wrong manner—in political action against Rome or in social segregation from "impure" people. Those who had been Jesus's friends came to the conviction that their leader was still alive and that their band was the body of Christ. They were steeled with the resolve to exemplify in their lives the values of Jesus. Hence, Easter commemorates the reanimation or rebirth of what was numb and broken, but it is something that happened to the corporate body of disciples, not something that happened to the corpse of Jesus. This resurrection awareness spread, as Paul suggests, from a single person, Peter, to a dozen disciples, who had also been remorseful when their leader died, to hundreds of others who knew Jesus less intimately.

The first letter of Peter provides strong support for Paul's outlook on the resurrection in 1 Corinthians 15. The consensus of scholarship throughout church history has held that it contains the thoughts of the apostle Peter recorded by Silvanus, as the letter states. Thus it may have been second only to Paul's letters in historical order of writing, and it may express memories of Jesus' resurrection that are some years earlier than even those of Paul. Brief though Peter's letter is, it contains telling verses confirming that the earliest apostolic testimony affirmed a non-physical resurrection for both Jesus and for Christians. After acknowledging that Jesus' role was that of the innocent sufferer described in Isaiah 53, Peter provides this contrast: "He was put to death in the flesh, but he was brought to life in the spirit." Regarding other resurrected humans, Peter states that "they live in the spirit as God lives."[39] Thus, according to the first person to experience Jesus' resurrection, Christians can confidently look forward to sharing more fully the immortal life of God after they die "in the flesh." Peter, who stresses the contrast between our corruptible earthly life and the "incorruptible inheritance in heaven"[40] is completely in accord with Paul's judgment that "this perishable nature must put on the imperishable and this mortal nature must put on immortality."[41]

During the generation after Paul's death his perspective of an altogether non-physical resurrection was virtually eclipsed

by a doctrine of carnal resurrection. The tendency to material-
ize the resurrection of the dead infiltrated the church and
became the normative interpretation in subsequent Christianity.

Mark, the earliest Gospel, was written about one decade
after Paul's letters. According to the two best New Testament
codices, Sinaiticus and Vaticanus, the resurrection account in
Mark's last chapter ends abruptly with the clause "for they
were afraid." The dozen spurious verses that follow in some
manuscripts are efforts centuries later to give the Gospel an
ending in harmony with the other Gospels. Also, believers are
there given the crass assurance that it will not harm them to
handle serpents and drink poison. Mark 16 introduces, for the
first time in writing, the Easter story of women at an empty
tomb on the first day of the week after Jesus was buried there.
Its concluding comment, that the frightened women said
nothing to anyone, was probably made to explain why the
empty tomb story was unknown to early church leaders and
emerged some time later. As a record of what actually happened, it is unlikely that women who were courageous enough
to remain at Jesus' crucifixion until his agonizing death (unlike
the male disciples), were fearful to tell others that his tomb was
empty.

The Gospel of Matthew, written about a decade after Mark,
adds to the story of Jesus' resurrection. In the last chapters of
that Gospel, guards are introduced to keep sealed the tomb
where Jesus was buried. They are foiled , however, by an angel
who rolls away the stone. Matthew also features a violent
earthquake on Easter morning and an appearance of Jesus in
Galilee as well as in Jerusalem. His corporeality is displayed by
the comment that his disciples "took hold of his feet" as they
worshipped him.

The quantity of Luke's embellishments are striking.
Whereas five verses in 1 Corinthians 15, eight verses in Mark,
and twenty verses in Matthew tell of Jesus' resurrection, Luke
contains no less than 51 verses. The young man in Mark who

provides information to the women about the resurrection becomes two angels in Luke.[42] The women, far from remaining silent, "told all."[43] Mark has no account of Jesus' appearances, but Luke tells of two on Easter Sunday in Judea. There is little consistency in those accounts, for Jesus is non-physical in that he can vanish out of sight but physical in that he has "flesh and bones" and can eat.[44] Luke has Peter and Paul both appealing to an alleged prophecy by David regarding one of his descendents' physical resurrection.[45] In his Pentecost sermon Peter proclaims: "David foresaw and spoke of the resurrection of the Messiah when he said, 'He was not abandoned to death, nor was his body destroyed.'" Actually, the Hebrew psalm quoted here has no reference to resurrection of any kind.

Realizing that Christians were no longer claiming experiences of Jesus' post-mortem corporeal body at the time when he wrote, Luke constructs a story to tell of the final disappearance of Jesus' revived body. An ascension relieved for him, and others accepting the ancient two-storied cosmology, the problem created by the restoration of Jesus to his former physical state. Introduced at the end of Luke's Gospel and at the beginning of Acts are the only New Testament accounts of Jesus' ascension at a time later than his resurrection. Paul considered Jesus' resurrection and exaltation to be the same spiritual reality.

The Fourth Gospel concludes with even more embellishments than the earlier ones. This is what would be expected in a record that dates nearly a century after Jesus' lifetime. John tells of burial clothes Jesus left behind in an empty tomb, establishing that his corpse had been placed there. Male disciples see the empty tomb, affording court acceptable evidence that Jesus' body had disappeared. Although the resurrected Jesus was ghostlike enough to go through locked doors, he encouraged Thomas to feel his crucifixion scars. Later, in Galilee, a materialized Jesus cooks breakfast for his disciples.

In the course of a few decades there was a strange reversal of the earliest traditions which Paul recorded. He had not mentioned an empty tomb, nor clutching disciples, nor angels. Presumably Peter and James did not know of such happenings either, for Paul had visited with them for two weeks in Jerusalem several years after his conversion.[46] Surely Paul would have learned at that time details of Jesus' physical resurrection, if such had occurred, and he would later have communicated to the Corinthians all the proof he had received from the apostles.

Whereas Paul, and perhaps the other apostles, rejected the resurrection of the flesh, Jesus' nail-pierced body is, a generation later, portrayed as able to assimilate food in a life-after-death. During the half-century when the New Testament was written there was a shift in epistemology, and this resulted in an increasing tendency to flesh out the picture of Jesus' resurrection that was held by the earliest Christians. Paul, on the one hand, affirms with total certainty that Jesus has risen but, on the other hand, has no concern to provide objective proof. He frankly admits that his doctrine of immortality is not based on sense experience. But the later Gospels offer supernatural evidence that is directed toward naive empiricists like Thomas who hold that only what is tangible is true and real.

James Robinson, in his presidential address at the Society of Biblical Literature, adroitly showed how the ancient Christian texts that have been discovered during the past generation support the assumption that the physicality of Jesus' resurrection in the canonical Gospels "reflects a secondary stage in the transmission of resurrection appearances." His analysis of early Christian writings demonstrates that what came to be accepted as orthodox Easter doctrine was established on a misinterpretation of the primary stage of Christianity. The church was launched not by the physical resurrection of Christ but by visions of a luminous spiritual body to which Paul refers. After those visionary experiences faded, apologists wrote of alleged objective happenings in an attempt to prove the truth of the Easter event.[47]

Each Gospel writer seems to want to outdo previous accounts in providing documentation of Jesus' alleged physical resurrection that would satisfy the common, naive empiricist. The frame of mind toward which Christian resurrection evidence is directed is reflected in the Apocalypse of Baruch. That Jewish book, written during the era of the Gospels, proclaims: "The earth shall then assuredly restore the dead which it now receives in order to preserve them; it shall make no change in their form." Baruch asserts that physical resurrection is "necessary to show to the living that the dead have come to life again."[48]

There is the tacit assumption in the Gospels that if the physical resurrection of Jesus can be accepted as indubitable, then the general physical resurrection of other humans is also certain. Thus Matthew asserts that in the aftermath of an earthquake at Jerusalem this happened: "The tombs were opened and bodies of the saints were raised from sleep. They came out of the tombs and after Jesus' resurrection they entered into the Holy City, where many saw them."[49] Again, John's Gospel portrays Lazarus, like Jesus, as being able to eat food after his resurrection.[50]

Post-New Testament Views

In his *History of Christian Thought*, Arthur McGiffert observes that, other than some Gnostics who were deemed unorthodox, Christians living after the New Testament era held a doctrine of the resurrection that was essentially opposed to Paul. He states: "Most of the early Christians interpreted it in materialistic terms as the resurrection of the present fleshly body."[51] McGiffert's one illustration comes from a second-century sermon: "Let none of you say that this flesh...does not rise again."[52] The molders of normative doctrine during that century are even more forthright. Justin declares: "Christians who are orthodox on all points know that there will be a resurrection of the flesh."[53] Actually he is the first to use the phrase "resurrection of the flesh." Justin believes that the mundane body will be exactly replicated.[54] Athenagoras puzzles over this question: how will there be full resurrection of the flesh for those who have been eaten by beasts and cannibals? He explains that organisms cannot assimilate food which is not a part of their natural diet. Human flesh can thus never become part of other bodies, so it is either vomited or excreted undigested. Then, in the resurrection, there will be a fusing together of the fragmented and decomposed bodies. Athenagoras concludes: "It is impossible for the same persons to be reconstituted unless the same bodies are restored to the same souls."[55]

The influential Bishop Irenaeus gives much attention to arguing against Gnostics who reject a physical resurrection. Basing their authority on Paul's assertion that "flesh and blood cannot inherit the kingdom of God,"[56] they hold that Christians err if they imagine that the rising up of a corpse has occurred for Jesus or for any of his followers. Irenaeus interprets Paul to mean only that those who are devoted to "the lusts of the flesh" will not qualify for citizenship in God's kingdom. He insists that Christians will be raised "in the same manner as Christ rose in the substance of flesh and pointed out to his disciples the marks of his nails and the opening in his side." From alleged miracles of the Old Testament and the Gospels the Bishop drew arguments he thought would buttress orthodoxy. The dry bones sermon in Ezekiel 37 is viewed not as a forecast of Israel's national revitalization, as the prophet explicitly states, but as God breathing life into scattered skeleton parts and revivifying individuals who had died. Irenaeus claims that Jesus restored crippled limbs and diseased eyes in order to guarantee sound bodies in eternity for those whom he healed. In the cases of Lazarus, the son of the widow of Nain, and the daughter of Jairus, "the dead rose in the identical bodies, their limbs and bodies receiving health" to prefigure the future resurrection of the dead.[57]

Apocryphal gospels written during the century after the canonical Gospels satisfied the growing hunger for more detailed information about physical resurrection. Nowhere in the New Testament is this question asked or answered: *how* did Jesus rise? There were none in the first century who claimed to have witnessed Jesus' exit from the tomb. That gap was partly filled in with this embroidery from the Gospel of Peter. Two men descend from heaven before dawn on "the Lord's day" and enter the sepulcher where Jesus is buried. Presently, the Roman soldiers and Jewish elders guarding the tomb see three men come out, "two of them sustaining the other, and a cross following them, and the heads of the two reaching to heaven, but that of him who was led of them by the hand overpassing the heavens."[58] According to the Gospel of the Hebrews, Jesus verifies his physical resurrection to the Jerusalem authorities by giving his shroud to the servant of the high priest before going to find his brother James.[59] Another apocryphal account attempts to confirm the doctrine that there was a physical resurrection for Jesus and that consequently there will be the same for all humans. These words are put into the mouth of the risen Jesus: " 'That you may know that it is I, lay your hand, Peter, (and your finger) in the nailprint of my hands; and you, Thomas, in my side; and also you, Andrew, see whether my foot steps on the ground and leaves a footprint. For it is written in the prophet, "A ghost, a demon, leaves no print on the ground." ' Now we felt him, that he had truly risen in the flesh."[60]

Tertullian, who did much to crystallize doctrine in the Latin Church, insisted on belief in flesh restoration of the wicked and the righteous.[61] In one treatise he has this to say regarding his admittedly irrational belief in the resurrection of Christ: "He rose again; the fact is certain because it is impossible." Tertul-

lian goes on to clarify that the resurrection doctrine has reference to "this flesh, suffused with blood, built up with bones,
interwoven with nerves, entwined with veins."[62] For a proof-
text Tertullian quotes words that Luke put in the mouth of the
resurrected Jesus: "Feel me and see that it is I myself, for a
spirit has not flesh and bones as you behold me having."[63] In
discussing 1 Corinthians 15, Tertullian does accept Paul's logic
that the resurrection for Christians is of the same type as the
resurrection of Christ.[64] Yet he opposes Paul in this assertion:
"The flesh shall arise again, wholly and entire in every man in
its identity, it its absolute integrity."[65] Tertullian interprets
Paul's claim that "flesh and blood cannot inherit the kingdom
of God" to mean that all humans will rise physically, but only
those who have been spiritually sanctified will actually "inherit
the kingdom."[66] The rest will be punished everlastingly. All
will have limbs restored that were amputated and teeth that
were extracted before death. The latter are especially needed
by the damned. Without such, asks literal-minded Tertullian,
how can Jesus' frequent prophecy be fulfilled that there will be
"weeping and gnashing of teeth" by those in hell?[67] This fanatic
went beyond the New Testament and grasped at anything
appearing to suggest that buried bodies retain their integrity.
The preservation of Jonah while submerged for days in the
digestive tract of a whale is taken for Old Testament evidence.
Also, he cites empirical data: some corpses that had been
interred at Carthage five centuries earlier were found to be still
sound, even to the extent of the hair retaining its perfume.[68] In
reference to Tertullian's resurrection doctrine, J.N.D. Kelly
has written: "This vigorous, full-blooded realism was to set the
pattern for later orthodox thought on the subject."[69]

The Greek and Latin antecedents of what we now call "the
Apostles' Creed" date back as early as Tertullian in the third
century. They all affirm: "I believe...in the resurrection of the
flesh (*sarkos* or *carnis*)."[70] Countless millions of Christians

across the centuries have learned the official doctrine of the church through a creed that many people wrongly presume was formulated by the apostles. Encouraged by this deceptive identification with Jesus' right-hand men, Christians have believed that scattered bits of dust will, in some unnatural manner, again become one's own personal organism when they move into heavenly mansions.

Origen, in the third century, was the only notable theologian in the age of the church fathers who completely accepted Paul's resurrection doctrine. He correctly points out that the apostle rejected a "flesh and blood" resurrection and championed a "spiritual body" resurrection.[71] When pagan Celsus attacked the doctrine of fleshly resurrection, Origen separates himself and his followers from the prevailing Catholic position. He appropriates Paul's grain analogy in his response: "We do not maintain that the body which has undergone corruption resumes its original nature any more than the grain of wheat which had decayed returns to its former condition."[72]

Strange as it may seem, Jerome judges Origen to be unorthodox because he accepted the creed of an apostle and rejected the term *sarkos* in the pseudo-"Apostles' Creed," written centuries after the apostles. Jerome classifies Origen among those heretics who claim that "the bodies that we shall have in heaven will be subtle and spiritual according to the words of the apostle: 'It is sown a natural body; it is raised a spiritual body.'"[73] The resurrected body must have a stomach, Jerome reasons; otherwise, how can the Gospels presume that Lazarus and Jairus' daughter ate food after being raised? That influential translator and interpreter declares that no physical parts will be lacking. Jerome states: "As our Lord rose in the body, which lay among us in the holy sepulcher, so we also shall rise again on Judgment Day in the very bodies in which we are now clothed and buried," John 20 implies. Jerome points out, that Jesus left his tomb with his teeth, tongue, palate, arms, chest, legs, and feet. Jeromne concludes: "The reality of a resurrection without flesh and bones, withblood and members, is unintellibible."[74]

Augustine, the last and most distinguished church father, believes that all humans will be physically resurrected.[75] "As for the substance," he asserts, "it shall be flesh, for after the resurrection, the body of Christ was called flesh."[76] Those who die in the womb as well as those who die at any post-natal age will be raised with prime-of-life physiques, because Jesus was resurrected when he was around thirty years old.[77] The restoration will be so complete that nails and hair will be intact, for Jesus promised that not a hair of our head will perish. God will "recall all the portions that have been consumed by beasts or fire, or have been dissolved into dust or ashes, or have decomposed into water, or evaporated into the air." Cannibalism, Augustine admits, causes the difficult question: who is the owner of the recycled flesh in the resurrection? In reply, the bishop pontificates: "The flesh shall be restored to the man in whom it first became human flesh, for it must be looked upon as borrowed by the other person."[78] As a celibate, Augustine recalls with guilt his former lustful life and is thereby convinced there can be no use of sexual organs in the heavenly "city of God." Specifically, female genitals will be transformed so that they will not provoke sexual desire.[79]

Understandably, interest in the preservation and veneration of relics was advocated by those who focused on the eventual reconstitution of the physical body by supernatural means. Among the early relic enthusiasts was Augustine who told fantastic stories of the potency of martyrs' bodies in curing illness and in raising the dead.[80] In the Greek Church there was such a craving for relics that some people were crushed to death in the press of the crowds wanting to touch the "holy body" of Basil before he was buried. It was considered meritorious to be killed in this holy pursuit, so those who died in the turmoil were considered blest.[81] In the Middle Ages much of religious life was centered in making pilgrimages to places where alleged miraculous bones were enshrined.

Aquinas modified little the traditional resurrection doctrine. "Christ's resurrection is the exemplar of ours," Aquinas held. Our imitation of Christ will even extend to our resurrection taking place before dawn. By definition, he claims, "we cannot call it resurrection unless the soul returns to the same body."[82] This belief in a physical reconstitution after death is still the official Roman Catholic doctrine. According to an Irish catechism published during the past decade, the resurrected person has "the same flesh made living by the same spirit."[83]

In spite of broad differences on other points of doctrine, the two principal Protestant reformers accept without question the Catholic doctrine of physical resurrection. Luther teaches that "our bodies, the same bodies that have died, shall be made alive."[84] Calvin follows Paul in holding that the resurrection of all humans will be of the same order: "When Paul says that we await our salvation from heaven, which will transform our vile and mortal body into his glorious body, he evidently affirms that the glorious body of Christ is not other or of another nature than the bodies of the faithful will be after the resurrection."[85] But the Reformer substitutes the authority of Tertullian for that of Paul in claiming that the corrupted corpses will be raised and will have the same elements of matter as before.[86] Early New Englanders expressed the Calvinist doctrine with this recurring tombstone epitaph: "God my Redeemer lives, and often from the skies/ Looks down and watches all my dust, 'till he shall bid it rise."

In the nineteenth century the Catholic Church's inflexible doctrine of physical resurrection precipitated a clash with the modern cremation movement. Canon laws were enacted to prohibit the burning of the bodies of Catholics and to deprive Church rites to those requesting cremation.[87] Those canons gave sanction to the unofficial condemnation of cremation

that had always characterized the Church. Until Christianity
came to Rome, cremation had been the normal Roman practice.[88] But by the time Christianity had become the state religion of Rome in the fourth century, cremation had practically
ceased and catacombs for inhumation were common. The
Church feared that cremation would diminish emphasis upon
belief in fleshly resurrection and in hallowed relics.[89] During
the past generation, Pope Paul VI eased up on the old restric-
tions by permitting church rites for those opting for cremation,
but he urged the faithful to abstain from the practice.[90] That
pontiff's relaxation on strictures against one method of corpse
disposal has not signaled a shift in traditional Roman Catholic
resurrection dogma. He reaffirmed that "souls will be reunited
with their bodies" on the resurrection day regardless of
whether the remains have been reduced to ashes or to dust.[91]

The Dogma of the Assumption of the Virgin Mary, pro-
claimed by Pope Pius in 1950 to be infallible truth, reinforces
the Catholic belief in physical resurrection. Alleging the
authority of Jesus and his apostles, Pius declared that Mary
"was assumed body and soul into heavenly glory" at the end of
her life, enabling her to sit enthroned as queen beside her son.
The dogma affirms that Mary was transported to heaven
without mortal decay. The faithful are instructed to find in this
compulsory doctrine a magnificent affirmation of the "lofty
goal to which our bodies and souls are destined." Whereas
their bodies temporarily remain in "the corruption of the
grave, she did not have to wait until the end of time for the
redemption of her body." This dogma is actually based historically on no more than the absence of reference to Mary's death
in the earliest traditions of the Church. Were this criteria for
assumption used for the apostles, for whom reliable death
records are generally absent, then it could be concluded that
they were swept up to heaven in a supernatural way similar to
what has been alleged of Mary!

The Mormon Church, a nineteenth century spinoff of apocalyptic Protestantism, has surpassed all Christian sects in interpreting the resurrection literally. That state is described in the Book of Mormon thus: "The Spirit and the body shall be reunited again in its perfect form; both limb and joint shall be restored to its proper frame, even as we now are at this time.... This restoration shall come to all.... There shall not so much as a hair of their heads be lost."[92] The wicked as well as the righteous will be physically raised, and the former will be "cast .into that lake of fire and brimstone."[93] The example of Jesus is cited by President Joseph F. Smith as the ultimate authority for this doctrine:

> He lived again in his own person and being, bearing even the marks of the wounds in his flesh, after his resurrection from the dead—so also a testimony has been given to you, in later days, through the Prophet Joseph Smith, and others who have been blessed with knowledge, that the same individual Being still lives and will always live.... We will meet the same identical being that we associated with here in the flesh.[94]

Eternal marriage will be provided for those who have been united in a special temple ceremony on earth, and innumerable heavenly children will be procreated.[95]

In tracing interpretations of the resurrection in Christian thought from ancient to modern times it has been shown that the doctrine has tended to become more materialistic with the passage of time. Initially some of Jesus' disciples were transformed through experiencing some visionary phenomena, coupled with some fresh insights on the mission of Jesus. From this certainty of an exalted Christ who was not defeated by his crucifixion, there arose stories of his revitalized corpse and his temporary return to have physical companionship with his disciples. Those stories were probably innocent creations by simple peasants to give material support for a reality independent of such verification. Those Christians, living after the first decades of the church's beginning, evidently found that reliance on apostolic testimonies of a spiritual resurrection could easily be dismissed by skeptics as the result of hallucination or illusion. They discovered that apologetics seemed to be strengthened when materialistic metaphysics was mixed with accounts of visionary experiences. Hence, some Christians came to believe and transmit stories of a sealed and guarded sepulcher and of a miraculous rolling away of Jesus' gravestone—presuming that appeal to alleged objective history would overwhelm unbelievers.

Throughout church history the best known and most appreciated accounts of Jesus' resurrection are found in the Gospels of Luke and John. Those stories, which were written down more than a generation after the events that they purport to describe, are cited as proof of the dogma that Jesus appeared to his disciples in the same physical body he had prior to his crucifixion. As has been demonstrated, this dominant view of Jesus' resurrection clashes with the earliest New Testament record written by Paul. For him the decisive evidence that Jesus had risen from the dead was not material. That apostle gives no basis for believing that Jesus returned to conditions of his earthly life.

The classic theologians of Roman Catholicism and Protestantism have followed Paul in claiming that Jesus is the model human and therefore the general resurrection for all Christians will be like his. However, other than Origen, churchmen prior to modern times have disregarded Paul's adamant rejection of a physical resurrection. The rank and file membership of the church has tended to interpret in a literal manner a phrase that Paul filled with symbolic meaning. When Paul referred to the "resurrection of the dead" he did not mean the "standing up of corpses," even though that is what the Greek phrase *anastasis nekron* literally means. Just as we commonly say that the sun rises when we know that is actually not the case, so when Paul

wrote about "resurrection" he was using a metaphor to describe the deathless life in the presence of God.

The prevailing tendency today is to accept what the Gospel
says about Jesus' resurrection but to endorse what Paul says
about Christian resurrection. Most Christians believe that
Jesus' corpse was revived at Jerusalem three days after its
burial and that it continued to have at least some of its former
physical qualities for a few weeks before ascending. Moreover,
many believe that this is an essential belief of their religion.[96]
This characteristic outlook is expressed in a contemporary
poem by John Updike. Its theme is that the church will fail if,
in Jesus' risen body, "the cells' dissolution did not reverse, the
molecules reknit, the amino acids rekindle."[97] On the other
hand, the typical Christian is less supernaturally inclined with
regard to her or his own body.[98] Unless he has been tricked by
the funeral home industry, which has vested interest in having
the client believe that he can take it with him, few Christians
seriously believe that the skeleton deposited in a casket will be
the bones that will arise and walk about in some future age.
Accordingly, Christians do not affirm "the resurrection of the
flesh" when they recite the "Apostles' Creed," even though that
was its original form. The substitute of the broader term
"body" for "flesh" in the English-speaking liturgy was no
doubt made in recognition that Paul distinguished the physical
body from the spiritual body and insisted that only the latter is
a candidate for resurrection.

It is an unintelligible nonsequitur to assert, as most Easter
sermons now do, that Jesus' physical resurrection and the
empty tomb are the basis for a non-physical resurrection of
Christians. For logical consistency, the assertion should be
either that the resurrection of the man Jesus was physical and
therefore the resurrection of his followers will also be physical,
or that Jesus' resurrection was spiritual and therefore Christians will likewise have a spiritual resurrection. To accept the

position stated in the authentic accounts written in the letters of Paul and Peter is to combine the historical truth of Jesus' spiritual resurrrection with a valid deduction pertaining to Christian resurrection.

To separate Jesus' life either before birth or after death from the general human condition poses a fundamental Christological problem. If there was a unique conception or a unique resurrection for Jesus that was categorically different from those of other mortals, how can it be said that Jesus was fully human like us? Even if Paul had heard a tale that associated miraculous conception of physical resurrection with Jesus, it is unlikely that he would have accepted it as true. The apostle would have perceived that such supernaturalism is incongruous with his conviction that Jesus was the expression of ideal humanity.

Plato once told a profound story that conveys his judgment that most humans tend to be metaphysical materialists. His allegory of the cave shows the plight of the masses for whom reality is what the senses report.[99] The cave prisoners represent percipients who find no validity in statements that cannot be confirmed by stimuli from an external source. They want to kill the Socrates-type who insists on leading them to a conceptual realm containing absolute beauty and universal justice. Paul likewise testified to a transcendent dimension of life that cannot be grasped by our commonplace three-dimensional perception. *Agape* is the term he uses to point to that dimension, and Jesus is the incarnation of *agape*. The apostle lamented that the "natural person," who rejects what is beyond sight and sound, misses "the things God has prepared for those who love him."[100] Authentic love, as Paul describes it, is a relationship between subjects, not between objects and subjects. The spirit of Jesus within gives conviction in a way that an empty tomb at Jerusalem or an image on a shroud at Turin can never do.

Paul's lengthy treatment of the resurrection in 1 Corinthians

15 has a significant ending. In effect he urges his Corinthian friends to turn their primary attention away from their hope for a future resurrection and from the past resurrection of Jesus. They should not seek Jesus behind them in history or above them in heaven. They are encouraged to devote themselves to the Lord's service in the present, with firm assurance that love's labor cannot be lost. Thus Jesus' resurrection is verified and death's sting is removed when Christians shoulder fully their responsibilities toward life, freely and openly sharing in its joys and sorrows. There is a grandeur in this dematerialized resurrection way of life that is not dependent on the anticipation of amino acids rekindling by supernatural intervention.

4

ASTROLOGY, ANGELOLOGY, AND CHRISTOLOGY

For at least as long as recorded history, humans in many global cultures have been fascinated by alleged astral deities and divine messengers. It has been presumed that those spirits have the power to forecast, or even determine, the successes and disasters of earthlings. Astrology and the occasionally related angelology has been associated with the rise and development of Christianity.

Ancient Speculations

Like all people, the Sumerians recognized that much that

makes for human happiness and unhappiness comes down from above. Some warmth and rain is essential for organic life, but too much results in disastrous droughts or floods. The Sumerians presumed that the resplendent objects seen in the sky controlled all the happenings in their Mesopotamian valley. Thus they made celestial observations and pondered their specific effects on daily life. Anthropomorphic characteristics were attributed to heavenly bodies, especially to the sun, moon, and the five visible planets, for they were constantly changing their position in accord with their self-determining personalities.

Some four thousand years ago the Babylonians took over Sumeria and adopted much of the Sumerian culture. Their ziggurat temples served as observatories for priests to follow celestial movements. The earliest concerns of the trained sky-gazers centered in the crucial sun and moon, but the planets and the more prominent fixed stars soon captured their interest. Marduk was associated with Jupiter, Ishtar with Venus, and Shamash with the sun. Divination was methodically set down after some knowledge of these personified bodies was obtained. For example, one omen text states that a lunar eclipse will bring destruction if it takes place in the first month of the year, but prosperity if it happens in the fourth month.[1] Out of simple predictions such as this, a complicated zodiacal system of mapping the geocentric firmament developed. The Babylonians readily accepted horoscopes, believing that the position of the heavens at the time of an individual's birth determined the person's destiny. The horoscope of one of them, found inscribed on stone, reads: "The position of Venus means that wherever he may go it will be favorable for him. Mercury in Gemini means that he will have sons and daughters."[2]

When the Persians conquered Mesopotamia, they carried on the astrology of the earlier peoples who had lived there. The magi (from whom the word "magic" is derived) of Zoroastrianism were deemed wise by those who believed that they could establish causal connections between the configuration of heavenly bodies and human happenings. Their prominence centuries later is displayed in Matthew's charming nativity story. According to that Gospel, "*magoi* from the East" followed a moving star to Bethlehem in search of the Jewish king it allegedly portended.

It was by way of the Greeks that Mesopotamian astrology made its way to western civilization. Plato, who lived shortly after the Persians had occupied countries in the Mediterranean area, probably learned through that contact about the astral speculation that Mesopotamians had evolved over millenniums. The Greek philosopher acknowledges that the first careful observers of the heavens were non-Greeks from the Near East.[3] Plato presents a three-tiered cosmic scheme that integrated astrology with angelology. In deference to his Hellenic tradition, he places the capricious Olympians first in the chain of beings. They actually function as emeriti deities because the second-ranked divine spirits who animate the celestial bodies are "the greatest, most worshipful and clear-sighted of them all." The regular way in which those immortals act signifies for Plato their sublime intelligence. Then, in third rank, come "the spirits and the creatures of the air" that flit about the earth. Plato advises that they "should be peculiarly honored in our prayers so they may transmit comfortable messages."[4] Since each airy spirit (*daimon*) is "intermediate between the divine and the mortal" it "interprets between gods and men, conveying and taking across to the gods the prayers and sacrifices of men, and to men the commands and replies of the gods." "God has no contact with man," Plato affirms, so the diverse spirits are "mediators who span the chasm which divide them."[5]

Astrology is involved in Plato's doctrine of reincarnation. The universe has souls equal in number to stars, so each soul is assigned before birth a star that reveals "the nature of the universe" and "the laws of destiny" to the one being instructed. Then, at death, the soul of the good man returns to its native star to prepare for recycling.[6]

After the Greek conquest of Western Asia, led by Alexander of Macedonia, "the conqueror was conquered." A torrent developed from the trickle of Mesopotamian astrology that had affected the cogitation of Plato. Classicist Gilbert Murray describes its impact in this way: "Astrology fell upon the Hellenistic mind as a new disease falls upon some remote island people."[7] The term Chaldean, which originally connoted a culture west of the Persian Gulf, now became identified by Greek writers with the astrologers from Mesopotamia. Theophrastus, a disciple of Aristotle, who lived at the beginning of the Hellenistic era inaugurated by Alexander, stated that "the most extraordinary thing of his age was the lore of the Chaldeans, who foretold not only events of public interest but even the lives and deaths of individuals."[8] In the third century, access to Babylonian astrological texts was simplified by Berossus, a Babylonian priest, who translated them into Greek.

Among the several Hellenistic schools of philosophy, Stoicism was most affected by the foreign virus. Zeno and his successors found the Eastern astrology a reinforcement of their belief in pantheism and fate. The Stoics admired it because it provided a universal framework for their philosophical theology. No longer did they need to appeal to local city gods as had been done in the traditional Greek culture. As Helmut Koester points out, the educated class found the astrology of the Stoics appealing because it appeared to be validated by the newly developing physical science.[9]

Astrology, which had been a spoil of war imported into Greece, centuries later became a spoil that the Romans brought back from their conquest of Greece. John Ferguson states that "this tyranny of superstition," which flourished in pagan Rome during the empire era, was fostered by the Stoics and Platonists.[10] On celestial movements, asserted Seneca, the influential Roman Stoic, "depend the destinies of peoples; the greatest and the smallest events are shaped by their malign or favoring influence."[11] The Caesars had astrologers among their advisors whom they frequently consulted on public and private matters. After receiving a favorable forecast from one astrologer, "Augustus had such confidence in his destiny that he made his horoscope public and issued a silver coin with the sign Capricorn under which he was born."[12] Emperors Tiberius and Nero were likewise addicted, and "Titus was haunted by his horoscope."[13] Domitian worried throughout life about a precise prediction by an astrologer of the hour of his death. When that day approached he executed some attendants in order to avert his doom. However, conspirators assisted this Caesar's fate by assassinating him on the hour he most dreaded.[14] "It was the Romans who most developed and believed in fatalistic astrology," observes Lawrence Jerome, "so by the middle of the second century A.D. emperors of the Roman Empire literally lived and died according to the 'dictates of the stars'."[15]

Historian Tacitus (55-117), who lived when astrology was at its peak in Rome, indicates that it affected the ordinary citizens as well as Caesar's court. "Most men," he admits, "cannot part with the belief that each person's future is fixed from his very birth."[16] Even Claudius Ptolemy, whose geography was the most scientific of ancient times, wrote a treatise in which astrological lore is presented as fact. He asserts that one's character is determined by the planet in ascendancy at the time of one's birth. For example, "Mars causes men to spit blood, makes them melancholy, weakens their lungs, and causes the itch or scurvy."[17] Vettius Valens, another writer at that time, states: "Fate has decreed as a law for each person the unalterable consequences of his horoscope."[18] Our terms lunatic, jovial, martial, saturnine, and mercurial are rooted in the Roman belief that the moon and planets affect human temperament.

In his study of the relationship between astrology and religion in the Greco-Roman culture, Franz Cumont states:

> Beneath the lowest sphere, that of the moon, the zones of the elements are placed in tiers: the zones of fire, air, water, and earth. To these four principles, as well as to the constellations, the Greeks gave the name of *stoicheia*, and the Chaldeans already worshipped the one as well as the other. The influence of Oriental religions, like that of Stoic cosmology, spread throughout the West the worship of these four bodies, believed to be elements, whose infinite variety of combinations gave rise to all perceptible phenomena.[19]

Mithraism, a mystery cult steeped in astrology, was one of the more popular religions in the Roman Empire. It was centered in Mithras, a solar deity who was worshipped by the Persians even before the rise of Zoroastrianism. According to Mithraic doctrine, a devotee's soul ascends by means of a seven-rung astrological ladder in this order: Saturn, Venus, Jupiter, Mercury, Mars, the moon, and the sun.[20] Each day of the week was marked by the adoration of one of those spheres.[21] A vestige of Mithraism is found in some of the names given in European languages for the days of the week.

Christianity moved into Rome at the time when astrology was at an epidemic level. Certain days or periods were presumed to have been designated by star powers as times when certain kinds of actions were approved or forbidden. Edwyn Bevan writes: "The fear of these world-rulers, particularly the Sun, the Moon, and the five planets, lay heavy on the old world. The Mysterious Seven held humanity in the mechanism of iron necessity."[22] The crushing fatalism that pervaded the pagan Roman culture caused persons to attempt to transfer decisions about the future to forces separated from the human condition. A flight from responsibilities and an authoritarian reliance on prognosticators accompanied the belief that destiny is predetermined by divine spirits who make celestial bodies their abodes. Ernst Zinner comments:

> Christianity was founded at a time when it was customary to consult astrologers and other fortune-tellers about any important decision. Men were caught up in a network of interrelations between heaven and earth and only the astrologers knew the correct relation. The latter for their part maintained that human activities were predetermined by the stars in their courses. Accordingly it was impossible for man to alter his fate.[23]

Shifting attention now from pagan to biblical culture, we find that the Hebrews tended to reject stellar powers and accept angelic messengers. The low status of the celestial bodies is suggested by the opening chapter of Scripture. There the almighty Creator is portrayed as creating the sun, moon, and stars to provide additional light. Since they lack a high priority rating, God does not get around to declaring that they should be created until the fourth day! The luminaries have exclusively a physical function, and are no more divine than the plants created on the day before or the fish the day afterward. They are controlled by the one God who hangs them as lanterns on the sky-vault, and in no way do they have power to control human destiny. Surely most ancient peoples would have regarded this theology as radical and would have been offended by its blasphemous attack on their primary deities. This rejection of pantheism and polytheism is a distinctive feature of Hebrew monotheism.

Other expressions of contempt for Mesopotamian star-god devotion are found in the Bible.[24] One indictment against Manasseh, to show that he was the most wicked of Judean kings, was that he "worshipped all the host of heaven." Living at the time when the Babylonians dominated western Asia, Manasseh participated in augury that was internationally popular but was prohibited by Israelite law. A Jewish exile in Babylonia offered this satire: "Let your astrologers come forward and save you—those people who study the stars, who map out the zones of the heavens and tell you from month to month what is going to happen to you."[25]

Jewish literature during the Hellenistic era claimed that Abraham of Ur rejected his Chaldean astrology heritage and recognized the futility of looking to the stars for signs.[26] It is proudly declared that the descendants of that patriarch have also refrained from "such things as witless men are searching out day by day" in "Chaldean astrology."[27]

With regard to angels, the Hebrews accepted much of the folklore that was common in Mesopotamian literature.[28] The Hebrews conceived of them as attendants of God, having sometime a human form and sometime an animal form. Since God was often thought of as a king, it was deemed appropriate for the heavenly court to function like earthly courts, with a number of administrators in attendance to advise the king and to convey his decisions to those of lower status. Angels were not objects of worship and were not associated with astral bodies.

After the Babylonian exile of the Jews, mediating angels were given a larger place because of "the increasingly austere transcendentalizing of Yahweh."[29] Accordingly, in the Apocrypha and the Pseudepigraph emphasis is placed on a gradation of named angels. For example, Raphael describes himself as "one of the seven holy angels who present the prayers of the saints and enter into the glorious presence of the Holy One."[30] Like a monarch's principal ministers, this archangel has direct access to his King. In this role he acts as an intercessor for subordinate beings and as a means through which the King reveals his purposes to them. The book of Enoch, written in the first century B.C., tells of archangels who are positioned closest to God's throne; they are encircled by "angels who could not be counted, a thousand thousands and ten thousand times ten thousand."[31]

Some of these angels were thought to be personifications of nature. The book of Jubilees lists "angels of the spirit of the winds, and the angels of the spirit of the clouds, and of darkness, and of snow and of hail and of hoar frost, and the angels of the thunder and of the lightning, and the spirits of cold and of heat, and of winter and of spring and of autumn and of summer."[32] The Jews who lived at Qumran praised God for nature angels in this way:

> When you stretched out the heavens...
> You also made potent spirits to keep them in bounds.
> Or ever spirits immortal took on the form of holy angels,
> You assigned them to bear rule over divers domains:
> Over the sun and moon, to govern their hidden powers;
> Over the stars, to hold them to their courses;
> Over rain and snow to make them fulfill their functions;
> Over meteors and lightnings, to make them discharge their tasks.[33]

The Qumran scrolls also tell of a struggle between two human armies under the command of two angels:

> All who practice righteousness are under the domination of the Prince of Lights, and walk in ways of light; whereas all who practice perversity are under the domination of the angel of darkness.... The God of Israel and the angel of his truth are always there to help the sons of light. It is God that created these spirits of light and darkness and made them the basis of every act, the instigators of every deed and the directors of every thought.[34]

Robert Grant concludes that Gnosticism developed out of apocalyptic Judaism, such as was found at Qumran. That sectarianism, in turn, owed much to Persian teachings about seven heavenly spheres under satanic forces.[35] Cosmic dualism was the main theme of Gnosticism, so the enlightened person sought escape for his soul from the material spheres governed by evil angels to the supreme God above.

At the dawn of the Christian era, Jewish philosopher Philo adapted Plato's angelology to monotheism. Philo posits that the remote God communicates with humans by means of mediating angels. This arrangement enables humans to withstand the "shuddering dread of the universal Monarch and the exceeding might of his sovereignty,"[36] and protects the Holy One from the defiling direct contact with the worldly. Philo interprets the account of human creation in Genesis 1 to mean that God made the spiritual soul while angels fashioned the physical body.[37]

Paul's Criticisms

Aggelos, transliterated "angel" in English, is commonly used in early Greek literature to refer to a human messenger, and Paul continues that usage in a few passages. He expresses appreciation to the Galatians for receiving him as "an *aggelos* of God."[38] It was not that the Galatians treated Paul as a discarnate spirit, but that they showed special consideration for him and were open to his disclosure of God's will. An *aggelos* could also be someone detrimental to the will of God. In discussing the deceptions of "pseudo-apostles," Paul comments that "even Satan disguises himself as an angel of light."[39] The psychological insight here might be expressed less figuratively by saying that evil can be rationalized to look lovely. Paul probably learned from earlier Jewish sages not to take demonology literally. One of them, Jesus ben Sirach, made this demythologizing comment: "When a godless person curses Satan, he really curses himself."[40] Hence, an angel of

Satan is for Paul a picturesque personification of an individual's evil tendencies, not a courier of a distinctive supernatural personality who rivals God in power. Actually, the apostle's only use of the phrase "angel of Satan" is associated with some mental or physical anguish which he calls "a thorn in the flesh."[41] Paul testifies that it was by means of that internal harassment that his religion was strengthened. When Paul profoundly describes the civil war between his higher self and his evil impulses, he makes no mention of Satan or the Devil. Neither in the Romans 7 introspective analysis nor elsewhere in his letters does he utilize the mythology that was characteristic of apocalyptic Judaism, namely the rebellion of some angels from God and their leadership by Satan after their fall.

In contrast to the prominent attention given angels in the literature of his era, Paul is remarkably restrained. It is only in his earliest letters that he employs such imagery from his apocalyptic heritage. In addressing the Thessalonians, he pictures the Lord Jesus descending from heaven with a retinue of militant angels who are directed by an archangel's trumpet.[42] As Paul's eschatology develops, he moves away from ascribing positive value to angels. In relegating them to an inferior position he did not, as did the Sadducees, regard them as non-existent.[43]

Paul's denigration of angels is apparent in several of his letters. In two of them he regards his understanding of Christianity as superior to what "an angel from heaven" might preach.[44] Far from having a status above humans, angels will be judged by Christians.[45] In order to indicate the inferiority of the Mosaic law and the superiority of direct guidance by God, Paul makes use of a legend in which the giving of the law is associated with angels.[46] After alluding to the so-called supernatural beings of his era, Paul affirms that there is only one Lord through whom all exists.[47] In his mature theology the apostle rejects any cosmological entity that might impose a barrier between the Christian and God. Christ, he claims, "delivers the kingdom to God the Father after abolishing every rule and every authority and power."[48] Again, he gives this assurance: "I am persuaded that neither...angels, nor rulers ...nor powers, nor height, nor depth, nor anything else in creation will be able to separate us from the love of God in Christ Jesus, our Lord."[49] "Height" and "depth" refers to astrological magnitudes determined by planetary ascension or declination. The "rulers" here refer to alleged star powers that Christ has destroyed.

When Albert Schweitzer examined the passages where Paul refers to angels, he found that the defeat of angelic power by Jesus' resurrection was an important part of the apostle's eschatology. Schweitzer recognized, as few other scholars have, that "Paul sees the Kingdom of God as meaning the overcoming through Jesus Christ of the Angelic beings who exercise a dominion alongside of and contrary to God's."[50]

Paul regards angelic and astral phenomena a danger not only because of the mediator role ascribed them, but also because they were thought to determine destiny. He refers to the Galatians' "enslavement" by the "cosmic elements" (*stoicheia*) prior to their liberation by the Son of God. The apostle is chagrined that some gullible Christians are regressing into observing auspicious days and thereby serving "elements" they consider to be divine. As we have seen, the seven astral powers were correlated in paganism to the week, with each power determining events of its special day. Paul writes chidingly about liberation from constricting astrology.

> When we were immature we were slaves to the cosmic elements.... But that you know God...how can you turn back to those weak and pitiful elements? Why do you want to serve them again? You are scrupulous about certain days, months, seasons, and years! I am afraid that my work with you may be for nothing....For freedom, Christ liberated us.[51]

Paul would have been unconcerned about the "ides of March" or any other days presumed to be ominous. He was acutely aware of the presence of evil in the world, but he maintains that the primary source was human misuse of freedom. Or, in the trenchant words Shakespeare put on the lips of Julius Caesar: "The fault...is not in our stars, but in ourselves."

Senator Cicero was among the few who were scornful of astrology in the Roman era. He wrote an extensive essay entitled "Divination" a century before Paul came to Rome. After showing the futility of a number of other popular superstitions—such as necromancy, dream revelation, forecasting from entrail examination, and prophesying by frenzied seers—he turns to an examination of astrology. Cicero respects the science of astronomy, which had predicted eclipses, but he deems "incredible madness" the claim that an individual's temperament and career is determined by the position of planets on that person's birthday. He reasons that twins should have the same degree of success, according to the magi's dogma, but generally that is not the case. Cicero concludes his devastating criticisms of astrology with this observation:

> Is it no small error of judgment that the Chaldeans fail to realize the effect of the parental seed?...No one fails to see that the appearances and habits, and generally, the carriage and gestures of children are derived from their parents. This would not be the case if the characteristics of children were determined, not by the natural power of heredity, but by...the condition of the sky.... The fact that men who were born at the same time are unlike in character, career, and in destiny makes it very clear that the time of birth has nothing to do in determining man's course in life.

Cicero, like Paul, did not intend to disparage rational religion. "Just as it is a duty to extend the influence of true religion," he wrote in "Divination," "so it is duty to weed out every root of superstition."

The Bible's only use of "philosophy" occurs in the Colossian letter to designate "worship of angels" and devotion to other "cosmic elements."[52] Paul bluntly evaluated that pursuit as "empty deceit" and scorns its concomitant self-mortifying prohibitions. A rigid and unhealthy moral discipline resulted from this assumption: that which is upward (in the pre-Copernican system) is pure and that which is downward and earthly is contaminated. To those who found that philosophy appealing, Paul inquires: "If with Christ you have died to cosmic elements, why should you be bound by rules that say: 'Do not handle this, do not taste that, do not touch the other?'"[53]

Those accepting the religious philosophy that Paul denounced, believed that the fullness (*pleroma*) of God equaled the summing up of many divine emanations.[54] They held that divinity was distributed in celestial spheres or heavens known as "thrones, dominions, rulers or authorities." Against that chain of beings, Paul boldly claims that "in Christ all the *pleroma* of Deity is embodied."[55] Thus, the planets and the moon, which were presumed to embody mediating spirits, could be disregarded.[56] Since the powers of divinity were incarnated in the earthly Christ, there is no need to focus on heavenly angels beyond, or even on the coming again of Christ in the sky. During his final decade of life the apostle no longer expected an immediate reappearance of Christ. The "glory" of Christ shifts from a heavenly spectacle to be disclosed *to* Christians and becomes a phenomenon *within* Christians.[57]

Grant sketches the way in which Paul's Christology has evolved to this point as he compares his first and last letters:

What is Paul doing as he writes to the Colossians? He is correcting their rather simple, though speculative, angelology by insisting on his own "realized" eschatology. In the course of the development of his own thought from the Thessalonian epistles to this point, he has come to lay more and more emphasis on the realization of eschatology and to think less and less of the future coming of Jesus. The Christian is one who "has been raised with Christ."(Col. 3:1)[58]

Post-Pauline Perspectives

Christianity of both the Gnostic and orthodox types accepted much of the angelic and astral doctrine that Paul rejected. The Gnostics believed in a series of intermediaries between the spiritual God and the material creation. For example, Basilides and Saturninus held that the "unknown Father" created a long chain of archangels and angels and assigned them spheres of dominion. The rebellious lowest ranking angels in that hierarchy made the earth, under the leadership of the God of the Jews. Consequently, the Father sent Christ to liberate believers from the dominion of the matter-makers and to guide their souls up the cosmological ladder to the spiritual realm.[59]

The last two books of the New Testament canon illustrate both the strong influence of apocalyptic Judaism and the slight influence of Paul's Christology in the church that developed a generation after his death. Jude is principally indebted to the bizarre book of Enoch, which contains an embellishment on the mythology in Genesis about divine beings siring giants by means of human women.[60] Enoch interprets the myth as referring to the primeval rebellion and fall of some angels from Paradise. Because they left their proper heavenly home, defiled themselves with lust, and engaged in unnatural divine-human intercourse, their punishment has been continuous imprisonment and fiery torture. The demons that have infiltrated the natural and social order are children of that illicit union.[61] After Jude relates to some of that Jewish folklore, it tells about archangel Michael contending with the Devil, and quotes as authority what Enoch records about the coming fierce judgment of the Lord.[62]

The book of Revelation, written about the same time as Jude, contains dozens of references to angels—far more than any other book of the Bible. Myriads upon myriads of angels surround God's throne above, and there are mighty angels standing at the four corners of the earth below, holding back its winds.[63] An elaborate mythology is presented in which Satan, formerly among the sons of God in the overworld, becomes, for a millenium, the chief of the underworld kingdom of evil.[64] The writer of Revelation delved into astrology as well as angelology. Illustrated in Revelation is the way in which at least one group within the church became the carrier of some pagan pseudo-science in spite of Paul's denunciation of stellar fatalism. In a scholarly treatment of astrology, Jack Linsay notes: "Early Christians could not easily disentangle themselves from the elements of astrology pervading their environment, especially those elements that had become imbedded in popular culture. Revelation is full of astrological ingredients as shown by the frequency of astral images and the stress on numerology, with seven and twelve especially prominent."[65]

None of the esteemed theologians of Christian orthodoxy have followed Paul in depreciating angels. Ignatius boasts that he can "grasp heavenly mysteries, the ranks of angels, the array of principalities, things visible and invisible."[66] Justin Martyr includes angels among those persons whom Christians "worship and adore." To them God committed "the care of man and of all things under heaven."[67] Bishop Ambrose advises Christians to "pray to the angels, who are given to us as guardians."[68] The tendency to exalt angels was temporarily checked in the fourth century by the Council of Laodicea, which prohibited the invoking of angels, calling it idolatry.[69]

At the beginning of the sixth century, angelology received a mighty boost with the publication of *Celestial Hierarchy*. It was authored by a Neoplatonic Christian who deceptively backdated his fantasy to a first century man named Dionysius the Areopagite. The fraud quickly obtained high authority because it was presumed that its writer was a biblical character who had obtained his ideas from an apostle. Acts 17:34 does state that an Athenian leader named Dionysius was among the converts of Paul. Pope Gregory the Great accepted the work as authentic, so from the seventh century until the modern era it was employed as a prime source of Christian theology, and the author was acclaimed as Saint Dionysius. Catholic scholar A.A. Bialas rightly claims that "*Celestial Hierarchy* is largely responsible for angelic cult becoming firmly and universally established in the church."[70] The treatise declares that God reveals himself only to the cherubim in the top triad of spiritual beings. Then, in succession, truth is disclosed to the seraphim and thrones in the inner sanctum. The chain of revelation descends to the dominions, powers, and authorities of the second triad and then to the principalities, archangels and ordinary angels of the lowest level. Reversing the bureaucratic chain of command, "inferior beings [humans] are to rise spiritually toward the divine through the intermediary of beings who are hierarchically superior."[71]

The impact of Pseudo-Dionysius' angelology contributed to the Seventh Ecumenical Council in 787 approving that angels could be venerated. Centuries later *Celestial Hierarchy* inspired the adoration of angels in the scholastic theology of the Middle Ages. Adolph Harnack, a leading church historian, comments: "As the Deity was farther and farther removed from ordinary Christian people by speculation, there gradually arose, along with the thought of the intercession of the angels, a worshiping of them."[72]

Thomas Aquinas was entranced by *Celestial Hierarchy* and accordingly wrote a lengthy and subtle treatise that enlarged on Pseudo-Dionysius' treatment of the substance and function of angels. Its popularity resulted in Aquinas being designated "the angelic doctor." His discussion of "whether several angels can simultaneously occupy the same place"[73] may have been stimulated by the proverbial scholastic question, "How many angels can dance on the head of a pin?" Due primarily to the discussion by that outstanding theologian, Mortimer Adler, editor of the *Great Books of the Western World*, has ranked "angel" as one of the hundred outstanding topics in the history of our civilization.

Dante, who gave a literary rendering of medieval Catholic theology, tells in *Paradise* of touring the seven heavens of classical astrology and of coming to three triads of angelic choirs. In that monumental poem he acknowledges that he was following the angelic arrangement set down in *Celestial Hierarchy*. Ironically for those who understand Paul's doctrine, Dante suggests that Pseudo-Dionysius angelology came from his mentor, Paul![74]

Pseudo-Dionysius' writings had an abiding effect on Christian vocabulary. Although the Latin term *supernaturalis* and its Greek equivalent had been employed in the ancient pagan culture, early Christians managed to explain their religions without making use of it. *Supernaturalis* did not make its debut in Christianity until it appeared in the translation of Pseudo-Dionysius' books. After Aquinas and other scholastics popularized the term it became basic for theological discussions in subsequent centuries.[75]

With the Protestant Reformation came a de-escalation in the adoration of all figures—be they earthly saints or heavenly angels—who might compete with monotheism. Although Protestant theologians accepted the reality of angels, most of them treat them as having little significance. John Calvin is probably a representative theologian in this regard. Regarding *Celestial Hierarchy* he makes this satirical comment: "If you read that book, you would think a man fallen from heaven recounted ...what he had seen with his own eyes!" Calvin advises his readers to "leave those empty speculations which idle men have taught apart from God's Word, concerning the nature, orders, and number of angels." That reformer contrasts *Celestial Hierarchy* with 2 Cor. 12:2-4, where Paul refuses to comment on the content of a celestial vision he had had. Calvin concludes his discussion of angels with this warning against idolatrous superstitions:

> Farewell, then to that Platonic philosophy of seeking access to God through angels, and of worshipping them with intent to render God more approachable to us. This is what superstitious and curious men have tried to drag into our religion from the beginning and persevere in trying even to this day.[76]

Most modern scholars would regard it silly to attempt to study angels seriously, and few theologians now give much attention to the subject. Even so, there lingers a great deal of belief in supermundane beings who are complete with halos, wings, and white robes. A 1979 Gallup sampling of Americans shows that 54 percent believe that angels are real and not imaginary; among persons who claim to take their religion seriously, 68 percent believe in angels.[77] Hence Bishop John Robinson may speak for his English constituency but not for Americans when he writes: "For most ordinary people angels merely add to the cocoon of fantasy and unreality in which the Christian Gospel is wrapped."[78]

In recent years Billy Graham has attempted to revive the notion of angelic warfare that is featured in the Qumran scrolls and in the book of Revelation. In his best seller, *Angels*, he encourages those who are preparing for Armageddon. "Millions of angels are at God's command and at our service. The hosts of heaven stand at attention as we make our way from earth to glory, and Satan's BB guns are no match for God's heavy artillery." Yet, "Lucifer, our archenemy, controls one of the most powerful and well-oiled war machines in the universe. He controls principalities, powers and dominions. Every nation, city, village, and individual has felt the hot breath of his evil power."[79] Graham tells of ten grades in the angelic hierarchy and claims that these hawkish and supernatural objects travel with an infinite velocity to engage in surveillance of earthlings as "God's secret agents."[80]

Astrology has not been as major a theme in church history as angelology, but it has had some distinguished supporters. There were professors of astrology in the Italian medieval universities under church control.[81] Even some of the theologians who accepted rational and scientific approaches to knowledge also endorsed astral fatalism. Aquinas, while finding no certainty in horoscopes, does find truth in astrology. He states:

> The majority of men, in fact, are governed by their passions, which are dependent upon bodily appetites; in these the influence of the stars is clearly felt. Few indeed are wise enough to resist their animal instincts. Astrologers, consequently, are able to foretell the truth in the majority of cases, especially when they undertake general predictions.[82]

The English scholastic, Roger Bacon, a thirteenth-century contemporary of Aquinas, believed that horoscopes legitimately associated the rise of the Hebrew religion and the Christian church with conjunctions of planets.[83] Some of the popes at the beginning of the modern era were enchanted by astrology. Before scheduling official functions, astrologers were routinely consulted by Sixtus IV, Julius II, Leo X, and Paul III.[84] Through the practice of astrology Urban VIII predicted the death dates of some of his cardinals. When they retaliated by predicting the pope's death date, Urban issued a *bulle* condemning the use of astrology in forecasting the time of death of popes and other rulers.[85]

Comets were widely regarded by Christians as prognosticators of slaughter and plague.[86] Callistus III was so disturbed by a "hairy and red" object that blazed across the sky—later to be called Halley's comet—that he set aside several days for prayer and fasting to shift the fated destruction toward enemies of the church at Constantinople. Having unsuccessfully launched a fleet of ships to save that city from the 1456 Turkish invasion, the pope hoped that the heavens would fight against the Muslims.[87]

Renaissance scholars, who were devoted to reviving classical learning, often championed the astrology that was a part of the ancient Roman culture. Bertrand Russell writes with regard to the Renaissance era: "Astrology was prized especially by free-thinkers; it acquired a vogue which it had not had since ancient times. The first effect of emancipation from the Church was not to make men think rationally, but to open their minds to every sort of antique nonsense."[88]

The perennial popularity of astrology is difficult to fathom. For five thousand years there has been no essential change in the way the sky is divided for the drawing of horoscopes, in spite of the enormous increase in empirical observations. Since this activity is pseudo-scientific it is understandable that astrology's rejection of the geocentric model on which the system is based should not disturb it. What is bewildering is the way in which otherwise intelligent and educated people throughout the course of history have accepted zodiac readings that are simply fraudulent and scientifically inane.[89] It is estimated that one billion people on the globe follow astrology to some extent. Consequently, thousands make a living out of it—many by writing horoscopes that give individual forecasts often diametrically opposed. Most newspapers have daily columns on astrology but few have regular columns on astronomy.[90] There is more interest in those who attempt to manipulate the universe so that it will cater to our subjective whims than in those who attempt to describe the universe as it objectively is. As Will Durant puts it, the masses have always been "more interested in telling futures than in telling time."[91] Precision of temporal measurement by astronomers is lame stuff when compared with information about events yet to come in one's own life, which can allegedly be supplied by those claiming godlike omniscience. George Gallup has discovered in one of his surveys that 29 percent of Americans believe in astrology. After publishing this and other evidence of "a high level of credulity among Americans," he concludes: "A high proportion, even among regular churchgoers, believe in astrology. At times it seems that Americans are prepared to believe almost everything."[92]

Millions of astrology believers also claim to be members of the Jewish or Christian religions, even though the practice of astral divination is condemned in both the Old and New Testaments. Abraham left behind the star-gods of the Chaldeans more than 3500 years ago to become the father of the Hebrew, Christian, and Moslem religions, and Jewish exiles separated themselves from Mesopotamian paganism more than 2500 years ago, yet there are still many in the Judeo-Christian culture who remain in Babylonian captivity.

During the past decade a distinguished historian of religion, Mircea Eliade, has made this observation regarding astrology in the United States and Europe: "Never in the past did it reach the proportions and prestige it enjoys in our times." In former centuries, he maintains, it was popular with the rich and powerful, but now the zodiac business has hit the mass market. The sale of astrology publication has been brisk and computers have been programmed to produce horoscope printouts. Eliade notes that this lucrative neopaganism persists in spite of the fact that the dominant theology of Western civilization has supported human freedom and has opposed astrological fatalism. He suggests that the fantastic enterprise has arisen in our technological culture among rootless individuals who long to become related to the entire universe. They seem to find grandeur in being part of a cosmic plan that is incomprehensible and preestablished, even though this makes them puppets pulled by invisible strings.[93]

It has been shown that Paul, the ablest spokesman for original Christianity, had little regard for superstition and magic. He rejected the residual animism that was found in some Hellenistic philosophies. Although he did not have the privilege of understanding the cosmos as astronomers now know it, he shared their scientific supposition that the "celestial" spheres are void of divine substance. The material world was for Paul a good creation of God and not a work of the Devil, so it would have been a slur on the Creator had he speculated about an army of good spirits fighting to free humans from the shackles of physical existence. The apostle pushed aside the ladder of supernatural mediating angels that was prominent in the religious outlook of Judaism. Also, he was not in sympathy with the pagan need for a hierarchy of spirit powers to gyrate the heavens, to control the natural elements, and to determine human "disasters" (literally, unlucky stars). The focus of Paul's concern was on the Son of God who became bloody flesh, and he believed that Christ Jesus was the only connecting link with Ultimate Reality. The main theme of the Galatian letter continues to have relevance to the many Christians who have been captivated by astrology. "For freedom, Christ liberated us," the apostle wrote, "Stand firm, then, and do not submit again to the yoke of slavery."[94]

5

SUPERMAN AND JESUS

From primitive times onward, humans have been aware of two types of happenings. First, many things have been found to occur in a predictable and dependable manner. Rivers regularly flow downhill and trees always grow branches and not arms. Religion has not been primarily associated with these ordinary reoccurrences, for they cause no anxieties. There are other happenings that we experience or hear others tell about which seem to be strange, irregular, and unpredictable. Journalists tell of persons who have been pronounced dead returning to life and report that certain individuals appear to have astounding psychic powers. These weird and mysterious happenings tend to make us insecure. Religion has generally been

127

associated more with extraordinary events that make us fear-ful. Some insurance policies reflect the prevailing human out-look. An "Act of God" is defined as some freakish event—such as an earthquake in eastern America. God has been associated not so much with ordinary nature as with super-nature. Thus, in the course of history, a person who was known as a man of God was often one who was presumed to have supernatural powers.

Supermen in Ancient Cultures

Humans have always been fascinated with tales of super-men. Accordingly, in the Old Testament some of the pivotal personalities have superhuman qualities. Tales are recorded of Elijah who miraculously supplied food at a time of famine and who restored life to a dead person. Then, on Mount Carmel, he personally slaughtered 450 prophets of Baal after beating them in a drought-ending contest, and he had enough energy left to outrun horses headed for a city many miles away. On another occasion Elijah showed his power by calling down fire from heaven that consumed two platoons of Israelite soldiers. Finally that ninth-century B.C. superman struck the Jordan with his cape and caused the river to part. After crossing the river he ascended to heaven in a fiery chariot.[1] Elisha allegedly performed food and healing miracles at least as incredible as his mentor, Elijah. Moreover, he once made iron float, and effectively prayed for an enemy army to be struck blind tem-porarily. There was no ascension of Elisha at death, but his relics were magical. When a corpse being buried in his tomb touched his bones, it revived.[2]

Jewish folklore shows that even the scriptural tall tales were not fascinating enough for some. For example, there is in the Old Testament a mild story about a great magician called Balaam. But in the synagogue, some added on this wild tale: it seems that Balaam, by sorcery, flew through the air to escape the power of Israel. A magician from the tribe of Dan flew after him, but Balaam soared through five layers of atmosphere and escaped to Egypt.[3]

There are stories in the traditions of other world-religions about holy men who soar through the air with greatest of ease. Muslims cherish the story about Mohammed's nocturnal journey on a winged horse from Mecca to Jerusalem and thence through the seven heavens.[4] In Hinduism it was believed that "the yogi can neutralize the gravitational pull of the earth and keep his body floating at any desired level."[5] Buddhists claimed that Gautama could dive down into the earth as though it were water.

In Greek mythology there is the famous story of Icarus, the first hang-gliding enthusiast. He managed to escape from Crete by attaching wings. But Icarus was, like many youths, overly daring, and he flew too high. The sun melted the wax by which his wings were fashioned, and he fell to his death in the sea. Then there was Hercules who bare-handedly killed a huge hydra and fierce animals. The most dangerous feat of that enormous Greek was to overcome the three-headed, dragon-tailed monster who guarded the gates of Hades.[6] Hercules acted on behalf of the gods to overcome the power of death. Gerd Theissen points out that exploits such as these were a distinguishing characteristic of Hellenistic literature. It was in the Hellenistic period that Nicostratus of Argos thought of himself as superman Heracles when he went into battle.[7]

Lucian, a Greek satirist living in the second century of the Christian era, introduced the term "superman" (*hyperanthropos*)[8] to refer to pretenders who claimed to do acts as astounding as legendary heroes had done. He lampoons the credulity of Christians and other simple people who are exploited by the charlatan who poses as a superman. Lucian records a number of instances of trickery, including an account of a sick man rising up and carrying his bed away after receiving magical words and gestures. He tells of an incantation that resuscitated a putrid corpse and of a Pythagorean who could walk on water "with ordinary shoes" or fly over it.[9] This last caper is similar to a story, recorded in an apocryphal book of the New Testament, of Simon the Magician who astonished crowds at Rome by ascending into the sky. On seeing this the apostle Peter prayed that Simon might fall and break his legs, and this allegedly happened.[10]

Supermen in Modern Culture

In recent years millions have seen the movie Superman and its sequels Superman II and III. It was nostalgia that attracted me to the film extravaganza. I grew up with *Action Comics*, a strip first published in 1938 when I was eight years old. The film triggered in me poignant memories of boyhood anxieties and fantasies. As a weakling who could not spring up to the high bar on my jungle gym, it was then marvelous to behold one who could leap over tall buildings. It was natural for him to do what appears to be supernatural to earth creatures because he came from the massive planet, Krypton, where the force of gravity was much greater. After hearing my parents lament over the Nazi threat to truth and justice, it was reassuring to read in the comic strip about the indestructible Man of Steel zapping enemies of "the American way." But, most of all, Superman supplied me with mythical images that I transferred to the founder of Christianity. I had what might be called a myth-understanding of Jesus! The Jesus of my youthful imagining was an almighty being who regarded heaven as his real home. This Prince of Glory came from "out of the ivory palaces into a world of woe"—to use a popular gospel hymn description. He knew everything about the world ages before he visited this planet masquerading as a man of flesh. His true procreator could be called Jah-El, that is, the Lord God, for Jesus only seemed to be a son of Joseph, the carpenter.

As I dredge up that early theology I realize that other wires were crossed between Jesus and Superman. I suspect that many other youths and adults who yearn for successful heroes have blended some of the Superman mythology with the stories of a tragic Jesus. A dozen years after his mysterious arrival from outer space, Superboy Jesus began his preaching career by denouncing scribes at the Jerusalem Temple. In the decades following, Superman Jesus, as a spy for the Kingdom of Heaven, sent back information to his Father about the behavior of earthlings. Secrets could not be withheld from him for his X-ray vision could penetrate people and buildings. However, he did not do miracles most of the time, and usually he was thought to be a meek but attractive minister. Like an ordinary mortal he sometimes prayed fervently for God's help or allowed bad guys to abuse him. But he could instantly switch on his supernatural energy without even changing his clothes, and exercise the omnipotence he had imported from Glory Land. Even as Clark Kent became transformed in a flash from a fumbling, mediocre reporter into a bloodless, metallic power, so Jesus could become an unflagging divine rescuer. For example, while he was engaged in the very human activity of napping on a boat to regain strength he was awakened by frightened fishermen and made aware of the raging tempest. Immediately he dispelled the stormy weather to protect his friends from drowning. I usually referred to this deity in disguise as "Savior" because he specialized in rescuing the helpless. Since Lois Lanes were always getting themselves into difficulties, this clean and square Prince was frequently a gallant protector of women. Of course he would never marry one, for such human indulgence would compromise his single-minded devotion to smashing satanic, un-American forces. He could not simultaneously give himself unconditionally to one person and protect other needy persons from misfortune.

Also, he knew from his Bible that giant offspring and catastrophe were the outcome when the sons of God were attracted to antediluvian women. If the genes of an alien from another sphere were mixed with those of a human, something as grotesque as Hitler's race of supermen might emerge.

Super-Jesus could vanish when the going got rough. Once when a hometown gang led him out to cast him off a cliff, he disappeared from the scene. However, like Achilles, Jesus was vulnerable in one way: he was not protected by his Heavenly Father from a cross. His enemies made the most of this, killing him after a bloody ordeal. Their victory was temporary, however, for he soon arose from the place where he was buried, rolled back the heavy stone sealing his tomb, and flew around Judea and Galilee. After entering for a moment in eternity into the atmosphere of planet earth, this dazzling dynamo lifted off from Jerusalem into outer space. I presumed that Jesus was now gliding effortlessly with raised arms in the blue beyond or sitting it out at the right hand of his father's gleaming white throne in the heavens, awaiting a second reentry. At the final Judgment Day he would descend from his orbit, knock out all Lucifer-like opposition, and gather up all reverential Christians to soar with him.

Some reviewers have also evaluated the movie Superman as a pop version of the Gospel. In an editorial entitled "Messiah in Blue Tights," Philip Jenks in the official journal of the American Baptist denomination urges dramatists who portray Jesus to learn from Superman, who "is a perfect balance of just-folks humanity and all-powerful being." Jenks asks, "If it came down to the ultimate competition, would Jesus or Superman win the academy award?" Neither does Jack Kroll, in his *Newsweek* cover story, regard Superman as a parody of Jesus. He recounts the episode of Lois Lane's resurrection by Superman through a titanic time-reversal of the earth, and then exults over that being a "great revelatory myth" for bringing back to consciousness "the Resurrection and the Life"—a title for Jesus in the Gospel of John.[11]

In a more sophisticated way, those reviewers champion values similar to what I heard a boy express at a church service. During the "children's time" the minister asked the youngsters assembled around him, "Who in the Bible do you most admire and want to be like?" "Jesus," was the first response. "Why?" asked the minister approvingly. "Because I would like to walk on water," was the reason given by the kindergarten child. For that boy it is likely that only Santa is superior to Jesus, for he can sail from chimney to chimney by means of his speedy airborne sleigh.

In the medieval folk-culture Jesus had all the powers now reserved for Santa and Superman. The Gospel of Pseudo-Matthew tells of the way in which Jesus, even as an infant, assisted his family in their journey across the Sinai desert:

> While they traveled on, Joseph said to him, "Lord, we are being roasted by this heat".... Jesus said to him, "Fear not, Joseph, I will shorten your journey, so that what you were going to traverse in the space of thirty days, you will finish in one day." While this was being said, behold, they began to see the mountains and cities of Egypt.[12]

The Human Jesus

How different are our Superman fantasies from the way the authentic early Christian traditions portray the human Jesus! It is significant that even in those Gospels which tell of God's presence in Mary's conception, Joseph is, without qualification, called Jesus's father. The only biblical description of Jesus as a youth shows him not as a bionic boy but as a curious student who listened to teachers and asked them questions. Jesus, like the boy Samuel, grew in a fourfold manner: intellectually, physically, socially, and spiritually.[13] In other words, he had a normal pattern of growth.

The New Testament affirms that Jesus was "tempted in every respect as we are."[14] Since sexual desire is powerful in humans, it can be presumed that he dealt with the problem of lust in the manner most acceptable in ancient Judaism—by becoming married not long after reaching puberty. Marriage was not an elective for rabbis, so in absence of evidence that he was criticized for not marrying, it is likely that Rabbi Jesus participated in marriage when he was a young man during those decades of biographical silence. Even Paul, in search for arguments to justify his de-married status as a missionary, admits he is unaware of Jesus' attitude toward celibacy and states that the other apostles were married.[15] Had Jesus been celibate it is amazing that this abstention would have had so little impact on those of his contemporaries who patterned their lives after his.

Jesus may have heard of stories of supermen who flew by supernatural power. Such awareness would assist in interpreting the early Q source tradition of his wrestling with the temptation to become an exhibitionist. On recalling a psalmist's assurance that angels will protect God's faithful from being hurt when they fall, he contemplated doing a spectacular stunt.[16] "What would be the reaction of people in Jerusalem," he may have thought, "if they were to watch me jump off the Temple skyscraper?" But Jesus, unlike Superman, rejected sensationalism. He realized early in his public ministry that, regardless of what his Scripture may have claimed, it is wrong to attempt to make a religious witness by defying the force of gravity. That force is not confounded, but confirmed, by fools who try to be an exception to the universal rule.

In Jesus' day it was popularly believed that holy men could change the weather, in imitation of Elijah. To encourage a life of pious devotion, the New Testament recounts these accomplishments attributed to that prophet:

The prayer of a good person has a powerful effect. Elijah was the same kind of person as we are. He prayed earnestly that there would be no rain, and no rain fell on the land for three and a half years. Once again he prayed, and the sky poured out its rain and the earth produced its crops.[17]

A century before the Christian era, the Jews associated a man named Honi with Elijah the rainmaker.[18] According to the Mishnah a superabundance of rain followed Honi's prayer during a time of draught.[19] Then there was a contemporary of Jesus from Galilee named Hanina ben Dosa who allegedly caused showers to fall for the sake of his own convenience. When that righteous man was caught in a downpour while walking home, he prayed that he not get soaked, and the rain stopped at once. On arriving home dry he prayed and the rain began again.[20] By contrast, Jesus knew that the natural order established by the Creator does not favor the good guys, for "he makes his sun rise on the evil and on the good, and sends rain on the just and on the unjust." In his Sermon on the Mount, Jesus also referred to floods and hurricanes as witnesses to the impartiality of nature's Creator—they hit the prudent and the imprudent with equal intensity.[21] The God that Jesus affirmed was active in the regular processes of nature, but not to give special preferences to some. Rather, nature operates independently of human "just deserts," so life-sustaining and life-destructive forces are no respecters of persons.

It is significant that Jesus' outlook on the relation between human needs and weather phenomena coincides with that of eminent men of scientific orientation who lived both centuries before and after him. Aristotle observed that rain falls without regard either to giving growth to a farmer's grain or to spoiling it on the threshing floor.[22] Sigmund Freud ironically held that religion cannot stand up against the scientific spirit, which holds that "earthquakes, tidal waves, conflagrations, make no distinction between the virtuous and pious and the scoundrel or unbeliever."[23] Jesus, while having a theological outlook sharply different from the pagan Athenian philosopher or the atheistic Viennese psychologist, nevertheless shared their observation of natural processes.

Among the teachings of Jesus in the Q source is also found his criticism of those whose faith rests on alleged miracles. He states:

> This is an evil generation: it seeks a sign, but none will be given it except the sign of Jonah. For as Jonah became a sign to the Ninevites, so will the Son of Man be to this generation. At the Judgment the Queen from the South will arise and condemn the people of this generation, because she traveled from afar to hear the wisdom of Solomon; and there is more than Solomon here! The Ninevites will arise at the Judgment and condemn you, because they repented when Jonah preached; and there is more than Jonah here![24]

Jesus here commends some Gentiles who were open to non-supernatural expressions of power and wisdom. The Ninevites repented because of Jonah's "sign," that is, his demonstration of God's power through preaching. Likewise, the Queen of Sheba was convinced by Solomon's wisdom, for neither Solomon nor Jonah performed supernatural wonders. Jesus lamented that people in his own day craved for miraculous proof more than for religious teaching, even though at some earlier times they did not demand such.

Jesus' declaration that "no sign will be given"[25] was so counter to the assumptions of the prevailing apocalypticism of his age that it had little impact. Not many years after he refused to perform a miracle to confirm who he was, the editor of Matthew distorted Jesus' teaching about "the sign of Jonah." Like most Scripture-readers, that evangelist could associate Jonah only with a big fish story of supernatural preservation.

Thus he added to Jesus' words: "As Jonah was three days and nights in the belly of the sea monster, so will the Son of Man be three days and nights in the heart of the earth."[26] This addition reverses Jesus' teaching about no miraculous proofs and utilizes the whale story to signify the unnatural release of Jesus' crucified body from the depths of the grave.

Luke records a parable which reinforces that Jesus did not think supernaturalism has any transforming effect on personality. A rich man in hell, so it goes, requests that he be resurrected in order to warn his brothers of what will happen to them if they persist in his attitude of indifference to human suffering. His request is denied for this reason: "If they do not hear Moses and the prophets, neither will they be convinced if someone should rise from the dead."[27] Thus Jesus did not think that individuals can be amazed into a lifestyle of ethical concern. According to his parable, those who are unresponsive to the social justice teachings of the Israelite prophets will not be converted by a display of supernaturalism.

Without intending his action to be a sign of his supernatural power, Jesus assisted some sick people. He pointed out that the therapy he administered was not unlike that which other Jewish physicians were giving.[28] He tried to make people aware of the psychosomatic causation of some sickness, yet he recognized that he was powerless to effect cures among any who lacked confidence that they could regain health.[29] Even though Jesus did not seek to be known as a healer, he and his disciples did gain some notoriety as faith-healers.

In contrast to the comic book Superman, the historical Jesus was no loner who operated apart from a community. He knew that individual healings have no permanent effects, for everyone who recovered from illnesses would eventually die. Thus he gathered about him disciples and trained them to carry on his primary mission of telling about the coming "kingdom."[30] Unlike healing, teaching can be transmitted from person to person and from generation to generation.

Over against the jingoistic Superman who aims at preserving the number one status of one's country, Jesus was an internationalist. Some of his countrymen thought that a leader of their people should promote the Jewish way by advocating an armed insurrection. But Jesus favored living in peace with the Romans and did not gratify those zealots who were working for a military revolution. The Gospels show that those adversaries of Jesus who were opposed to "truth and justice" were more often fellow Jews than foreigners. Jesus was a social revolutionary who, like Isaiah's "Light to the Nations," aimed at bringing justice to his nation and other nations, but without blustering violence.[31] Far from attempting "to quench the flickering light" of particular Gentile and Jewish women and men whom he encountered, he fanned to brightness their assertiveness for worthy concerns.

The early Christians believed that Jesus showed his kinship to God when he was in no way manifesting irresistible physical power. A splendid illustration of this is seen in the climax of the passion account of the Gospel of Mark. Some Jews at the crucifixion, who assumed that power was best displayed in supernatural interventions, shouted this challenge to Jesus: "Save yourself, and come down from the cross!" They laughed at him, saying, "He saved others; he cannot save himself." Jesus responded with cries of agony and abandonment. The bloody victim was not, even emotionally, a "man of steel." Even so, a pagan centurion who witnessed this death scene exclaimed: "Truly this man was God's son!"[32]

As we have seen, there is no indication that Paul, the earliest known Christian writer, thought of the Christian life as a matter of putting one's "hand in the hand of the man who walked on the water." Paul held that even though many crave for happenings that go against nature, the true miracle of God is seen in the life and death of the lowly, loving Jesus. After listing human hardships in his letter to the Romans, the apostle does not promise that famine and war will be replaced by abundance and peace, but that no deprivation "will be able to separate us from the love of God in Christ Jesus our Lord." Elsewhere in Romans the incarnation of *agape* is expressed in this way: "God shows his love for us in that while we were sinners, Christ died for us."[33] Since the Crucified One is the quintessential personification of divine *agape*, a paragraph from 1 Corinthians 13 may be read with this substitution of subject:

> Jesus is patient and kind. He is not jealous; neither is he ostentatious, nor snobbish, nor rude. Jesus is not selfish; neither is he touchy, nor resentful; he does not gloat when others go wrong—on the contrary, he is gladdened by goodness. Jesus is cautious in exposing; he is eager to believe the best, always hopeful, conquering through endurance.

Some Christian interpreters from different cultures and centuries have grasped well the paradox of Jesus' power. For example, Martin Luther has observed: "On the cross Christ was powerless, yet there he performed his mightiest work."[34] Ian Siggins notes that Luther regarded the miracles of Jesus as incidental: "Miracles themselves are the least significant of Christian works, for the devil was defeated by weakness, not magnificent miracles."[35] Japanese writer Shusaku Endo has ably summed up Jesus' most profound effect on his disciples. That anti-superman

> possessed no power in this visible world.... It was nothing miraculous, but the sunken eyes overflowed with love more profound than a miracle. And regarding those who deserted him, those who betrayed him, not a word of resentment came to his lips.... That's the whole life of Jesus. It stands out clean and simple, like a single Chinese ideograph brushed on a blank sheet of paper.[36]

Jesus was super as in *super*lative but not as in *super*natural.

He was for Paul the superlative model of love. Showing *agape* to neighbors far and near rather than being agape at the fantastic was for that apostle the proper response to the Christian revelation. Gaping at the alleged supernatural has been a staple of folk religion throughout history, but the more demanding regulation of life by the principle of suffering love has not been so popular.

The writer of the letter to the Hebrews affirms that Jesus was superior to the mythological angels, in part because "he learned from what he suffered what it means to obey." Holy Jesus, like the Holy Bible, was a product of human environment and divine inspiration. Had he been a freak, ascending over cities, it would have been absurd for the New Testament to advise: "You should follow in his steps."[37] Such an Omnipotence may be marveled at but not imitated. Jesus was not a half-God, half-man hybrid; he was even more of a full-fledged person than his followers. To become like him is to discover what being human really means.

A poem of Frederic Myers relates in an exquisite manner the paradoxical and divine qualities of Jesus:

> Not as one blind and deaf to our beseeching,
> Neither forgetful that we are but dust,
> Not as from heavens too high for our up-reaching,
> Coldly sublime, intolerably just:—
> Nay but thou knowest us, Lord Christ thou knowest,
> Well thou rememberest our feeble frame,
> Thou canst conceive our highest and our lowest,
> Pulses of nobleness and aches of shame....
> Jesus, divinest when thou most art man![38]

CONCLUSION

It should be fully apparent by now that Paul's theology, as contained in his own writings, is the centerpiece of this study. It has been shown that he did not present Jesus as involved in supernatural miracles and that he did not accept the claims of such that were beginning to be circulated by some Christians who opposed him during the period of his missionary travels. In the chapters devoted to two parts of church doctrine which have been traditionally exalted and are still basic to Christian fundamentalism—namely, Jesus' alleged virginal conception and physical resurrection—it was demonstrated that Paul did not support either. Then, in the last two chapters it has been argued that his Christology stands in sharp contrast to magical views of the universe that have been perennially popular.

Paul's nine or ten letters, which chronologically precede the other "books" of the New Testament, are the only writings with undoubted apostolic authority. Standing at the head-water of the stream of Christianity, Paul describes, and to some extent directs, its flow during the crucial first generation of the church. However, from that vantage point he was unable to perceive the preeminent role that he was playing. Paul's self-evaluation that he was "least of the apostles"[1] shows that a person is often an unreliable judge of his own significance. He illustrates Jesus' paradox that "the last will become first." As the author of one-fourth of the books of the New Testament, he provides the only firsthand source of earliest Christianity written by a main leader. Thanks to the self-revealing quality of Paul's letter, there is no personality who is better known in ancient times than the one whom he calls "a man in Christ."[2]

At pivotal periods in church history, Paul's influence has been heavy. If Peter is excepted, Paul's impact has been greater than that of all the other apostles put together. The complex forces found in Paul's life provided Augustine with a model for integrating the intellectual and emotional aspects of his personality. Accordingly, his monumental *Confessions* and *City of God* are each filled with hundreds of quotations from Paul's letters—many times the citations from any other writer. A millennium later the Protestant Reformation was ignited by Luther's study of Paul's letters. That rediscovery continued with Calvin, who quoted from Paul's letters in his *Institutes of the Christian Religion* more often than from all four of the Gospels. Even though Augustine and the Reformers were guided by Paul, they did not, as we have seen, follow Paul fully in their interpretations. In our century the writings of St. Paul have been shown to be no more extinct than the mountain of St. Helens. His ideas have again blazed forth and are transforming the theological landscape. By means of persons who have been greatly influenced by Paul—such as Paul Tillich, Karl Barth, Rudolf Bultmann, and Hans Küng—modern culture has been given a dazzling glimpse of what is at the core of authentic, historic Christianity.

Paul's letters contain the gospel in its purest form because
they lead us closer to the essence of earliest Christianity.
Indeed, there is only one gospel in the New Testament that is
explicitly associated with an apostolic author. "According to
my gospel"[3] was a phrase used by Paul long before the Gospels
were written and, in two cases, attributed to apostolic authors.
Most of the uses of the term "gospel" in the New Testament are
not in the Gospels, but in Paul's letters. For example, Paul
announces at the beginning of Romans that his main theme is
the "power of the gospel."

Paul's interpretation of Christianity has been treated as
normative and has been used to measure the supernatural
deviations in writings later produced by the church, the most
important of which are contained in the New Testament. He
provides the only glimpse of the historical Jesus before legendary trappings had much chance to develop. Unlike most other
New Testament writers, Paul had no interest in attempting to
authenticate Christianity by unnatural happenings and, as we
have seen, he was critical of those who claimed that such
miracles added grandeur to Christianity. One will search in
vain in his writings for whimsical acts such as creating food out
of nothing to provide a free meal for a few thousand: but one
can find a teaching on economic quality that has resulted in
policies that have provided for millions of needy people. Even
though Paul believed that Jesus had the status of the divine
Lord of his Jewish heritage, he implicitly rejected an asexual
incarnation miracle. In commenting on the goods of God's
creation, Paul affirmed that nothing is unclean.[5] Hence, the
notion that sexual intercourse is defiling and that a completely
sinless person must therefore be conceived in a non-sexual
manner, would have been viewed by him as both blasphemous
and absurd.[6] Likewise, the apostle stressed the centrality of
Jesus' resurrection while explicitly rejecting that it involved a
reanimation of "flesh and blood." Paul believed that the Christian's physical body is like a fragile "earthenware jar" that is

shattered irretrievably by death. However, it has the redeem-
ing quality of being animated by the immortal "life of Jesus."[7]

The glorious cosmic sovereignty of Jesus eclipsed for Paul
the perennial ancient preoccupation with stellar powers and
angelic mediators. The force by which Jesus ruled was not that
of an amoral Homeric demi-god, drunk with the ability to do
magic. In condemning the "worship of angels" and "cosmic
elements" Paul advocates allegiance to the cosmic ruler and to
the moral principles of his rule. The apostle writes of Christ
and of the Christian life in this manner:

> In his humanity the full content of Deity lives, and in union
> with him you have been brought to fullness of life. Every power
> and authority in the universe is under his rule...As God's
> beloved and consecrated people, clothe yourselves with com-
> passion, kindness, humility, gentleness, and patience. Be toler-
> ant with one another and forgive one another as the Lord has
> forgiven you. And to all these qualities add love, which binds
> all things together in perfect unity.[8]

Unfortunately, the parts of the New Testament were not
arranged, as were the three parts of the Hebrew Scriptures,
according to the time when they were accepted as authorita-
tive. Paul's letters would then have the priority in the New
Testament that the Pentateuch has in the Old. Those letters
were the first Christian writings to attain a status equal of the
Hebrew Scriptures.[9] Within several decades of Paul's death his
letters were gathered from the churches to whom they were
addressed. They were then circulated together and this enabled
Christians to quote from them before the end of the first
century. That epistolary corpus became the nucleus of what
emerged by the end of the second century as the New
Testament.

If the books of the New Testament had been published in
their approximate chronological order, with the four Gospels

following the letters containing Paul's gospel, a different perspective toward the supernatural might have emerged. In Paul's gospel, "faith to move mountains" is depreciated and *agape*, an uncommon term in the Gospels, is exalted. The power of love, not the love of power, is the theme of the theology of Paul. He shows that all things are *not* possible to one who believes. He would have treated as foolishness, not faithfulness, a conviction that a loved one who had died could return from the grave in a tangible physical body. Had Paul heard of a tale of a decomposing Lazarus being reanimated, he would probably have regarded it as ghoulish superstition. He believed that a main purpose of religion was to change the attitude of participants toward natural happenings rather than to change adverse external conditions.

When scientifically oriented persons begin to read the New Testament according to the traditional arrangement of its books, they might quickly lose their motivation to venture further. On the basis of its opening chapters they might judge that Christianity is based on irrational supernaturalism. In the first chapter of Matthew a genealogy tracing Joseph's ancestors through Hebrew history is immediately made irrelevant by an angel's declaration that Mary, his betrothed, had become pregnant without having had intercourse with any man. The writer of that chapter and the one following presumes that divine guidance is mainly communicated through dreams. The second chapter of the first Gospel reads like bizarre fantasy when it tells of some Mesopotamian horoscope devotees following a moving star that came to rest over the house where Mary's child lay. Some translators have given their endorsement to the Christmas *magoi* by calling them "wise men" and not "magicians," as they literally and properly translate the term elsewhere in the New Testament. The incredible supernaturalism of Matthew's nativity story—virginal conception, dream revelations, and astrological portents— might well cause twentieth-century readers to conclude that one must deny science and reason in order to accept the gospel message. Matthew's prologue to the story of the adult Jesus sets the stage for dozens of miracles that follow. They portray a deity with a split personality. There is, on the one hand, a creator who is responsible for the orderly cosmos and, on the other hand, there is a supermagician who operates outside of his established framework in order to make people marvel.

If persons with scientific dispositions were to begin their investigation of Christianity with Paul's letters, they would probably realize that it is altogether possible to accept Christian theology without the sacrifice of intellectual integrity. Along with the scholarly Albert Schweitzer they might come to see that "Paul is the patron saint of thought in Christianity."[10] They would find that the apostle stressed that Christianity should engage one's whole self, brains included. To those Corinthians who were exaggerating emotionalism, Paul testified that "both spirit and mind" are needed.[11] To Christians in Rome he urged "rationality" (*logos*) in religion. Paul added to this exhortation in Romans 12 a mind (*nous*) renewal plea. *Logos* and *nous* had long been favorite terms of Greek scientists and philosophers.

Paul's distinctive mentality, combined with his urbane upbringing, explains why he was uninterested in miracle stories. Gerd Theissen has shown that the "primitive Christian miracle stories are rooted in the predominantly rural world of Galilee."[12] They appealed to the simple peasant and fisherfolk who shared the naivete of the less educated. The socio-cultural dimension of Paul's life was quite different. He was city oriented and received the best education that could be obtained in Judaism.

Some philosophers have admired Paul's appreciation of reasoned discourse. Several centuries ago Spinoza contrasted Paul with the prophets of his Hebrew religion. Unlike those who were continually proclaiming that they were God's spokesmen, the apostle occasionally acknowledged that he was uttering his own opinions. To illustrate that Paul thought of himself as a teacher and preferred intellectual argumentation to authoritarian prophecy, Spinoza quotes this sentence from a passage in the Corinthian correspondence: "I speak to you as sensible people; judge for yourselves what I say." Spinoza concludes with this hope for the modern age: "None of the apostles philosophized more than did Paul....How blest would our age be if it could witness a religion freed also from all the trammels of superstition!"[13]

Contemporary philosopher Frederick Ferré maintains that Paul places "unequivocal priority on the use of intellect" when he affirms: "I would rather speak five words with my mind, in order to instruct others, than thousands of ecstatic words. Friends, stop being childish in your understanding. Be as infants in evil but be mature in your thinking."[14] Ferré is convinced that it has been Paul's interpreters rather than the apostle who have created an impasse between religion and reason by associating the intellect with cold lovelessness.[15]

Paul's mature thinking is best displayed in his famous ode to love in Corinthians 13. There he depreciates "speaking in tongues" and acknowledges the fragmentary quality of human knowledge. Regarding theological knowledge, Paul is intellectually modest. He does not think it is possible to have the whole truth of God on this side of death. He admits that we now know only partially and "see blurred reflections." He hopes that some day "we shall understand God as completely as he understands us," enabling us to replace our glimpses of the truth with a complete vision. However, we live at present by "faith, hope, and love," not by absolute certainty. In his acceptance of openness, Paul set a high standard for Christian scholars. He has one central commitment: "God was in Christ reconciling the world to himself."[16] Armed with this he could face the dilemmas of life in an exploratory manner, risking vulnerability.

Paul's outlook can be clarified by contrasting it with Tertullian's uncompromising stance. Living more than two centuries after Paul, he did much, as we have seen, to establish orthodoxy in the Latin Church. "We have no more need for curiosity since Jesus Christ," he asserts; "nor for inquiry since the Gospel."[17] Tertullian presumes that the Bible contains all truth so there is now no reason for further questioning and research. Since God has finally revealed the truth, affirmation of it and obedience to it is all that is needed. Some of his rigid positions, such as that of the resurrection of the flesh, have held sway throughout most of church history. In this century there are many inside and outside of fundamentalism who continue in Tertullian's belief that experience as apprehended in the sacred and secular realms is entirely different. Roger Rosenblatt, the *Time* essayist mentioned at the beginning of this book, agrees with Tertullian that scholarly Athens and holy Jerusalem are opposing cultures.[18]

If Paul were able to express today his respect for what is reasonable, he would probably regard the story of Elijah soaring skyward in a chariot drawn by fiery horses as on a par with lore about Santa sailing from roof to roof in a sleigh drawn by reindeer. Spectacular stories such as these have always delighted the credulous, but the apostle expected adults to be wary of fantasy. Although he patiently nursed some "babes in Christ," he longed for Christians who could chew and digest "solid food."[19] He wanted people who could analyze the dilemmas of life in a Christlike manner and then act on their judgments in responsible ways.

Paul acknowledges that throughout history humans have learned of God by gaining understanding of natural phenomena. "To the eye of reason," Paul asserts, "God's everlasting power and deity have been visible ever since the creation of the world in the things he has made."[20] In line with Paul's philosophical theology, Francis Bacon holds that "God never wrought miracles to convince atheism, because his ordinary works convince it."[21] This outlook has been stated differently in our time by Jewish novelist Isaac Singer: "The most wonderful miracle is what Spinoza called the natural order of things. To me, causality is more than a category of pure reason. It is the essence of creation."[22]

Blaise Pascal, the pioneering French physicist, had an outlook similar to Paul in that he balanced in a subtle way the scientific and religion modes of perception. This aphorism of Pascal expresses a Pauline sentiment: "Two extremes: to exclude reason, to admit reason only." Paul found among the Greeks some who thought reason was all that was needed. To them he says: "Knowledge puffs up, but love builds up. If any one imagines that he knows something, he does not know as he ought to know."[23] The apostle was convinced that modesty toward knowledge was the disposition needed for dealing with all things. The providence of God, for example, was more than Paul could conceptualize. He exclaims: "How unsearchable are his judgments and how inscrutable his ways!"[24] This awareness of transcendence is articulated succinctly by Pascal: "Faith indeed tells what the senses do not tell, but not the contrary of what they see. It is above them and not contrary to them."[25]

The scientific habit of Paul's mind is well expressed in his correspondence with the Christians at Thessalonia. "Test everything," he asserts. "Hold fast to what is good." In another letter he urges them "not to be easily confused in mind or excited" about a particular matter and offers this general advice: "Let no one delude you in any way."[26] The apostle was aware that false pronouncements abound, so only substantiated assertions should be accepted. Paul's skepticism was akin to that of medieval theologian Abelard, who said: "By doubting we are led to inquire, and by inquiring we perceive the truth."[27] Far from confusing credulity with faith, Paul presumed that a Christian would not believe unsupportable claims. Armed then with his respect for critical judgment and with his understanding of the essence of the gospel, the inquirer could then attempt to separate what Jesus actually did and said from the out-of-character accretions in later writings by Christians.

The gospel according to Paul features the historical Jesus not as a master magician but as a moral teacher and as a companiable leader. The apostle transmits practical judgments of Jesus and records words he spoke to his disciples at the Last Supper.[28] The words, "This is my body," by which Jesus instituted the Eucharist had the most powerful influence on subsequent history of any he ever uttered, but they were not intended to be interpreted, as they later were, as a magical formula of transubstantiation.

Paul was confronted with a power-crazed Roman culture similar to our own. The Roman government thought of power in terms of building armies, crushing enemies, levying taxes, constructing roads, and erecting impressive public monuments. Power is also a basic word in our vocabulary: we speak of military power, electrical power, nuclear power, political power, industrial power, and the like. Paul took over a widely revered concept and transformed it to refer to what most would call powerless. To use Charles Raven's paraphrase, Paul says: "The Jews seek after miracles; they are beset with an idea of God as a God of power, a Sultan, a miracle worker.....We see God in terms of a man on a cross, of the love that suffers, and suffering redeems."[29] In addressing the Corinthians, Paul focuses on "the supreme power of God" but associates it with these undesirable conditions:

> We are often troubled, but not crushed; bewildered, but not despairing; persecuted, but not forsaken; knocked down, but not knocked out....We are continually in danger of death on account of Jesus, in order that his life may be seen in this mortal body of ours.[30]

Paul experienced this paradoxical power in a personal way

when he prayed to be relieved of a "thorn in the flesh" that was paining him. The response Paul received from the Lord became the core of his religion: "My grace is all you need; power comes to its full strength in weakness."[31] In some ways Paul's situation paralleled that of Job who felt that he was being unjustly destroyed by the arrows of adversity. While in the midst of overwhelming suffering and humiliation he poured out tears and prayers to God, acknowledging that he had benefitted from God's love in the past. In the end Job realized that such divine companionship was sufficient even when personal desires are unfulfilled. Paul's agony likewise echoes that of Jesus who "offered up prayers and requests, with loud cries and tears to God, who could save him from death," yet "learned through his suffering to be obedient."[32]

Judging from a letter of Peter, other apostles dealt with afflictions in much the same way as Paul did. By appealing to the undeserved sufferings of Jesus, Peter encouraged Christians who were undergoing a "fiery ordeal." The power transmitted by that apostle did not come from one who averted bad happenings by doing wonders, so Peter does not mention Jesus' alleged miracles. Nor does he appeal to a God who supernaturally effects virginal conception and physical resurrection, or who intervenes in the natural order to save the innocent from persecution. Rather, Peter finds power in the bloody cross and urges Christians to follow in the steps of the Crucified One.[33] By participating gladly in the sufferings of Jesus and holding unfailing *agape* for one another, Christians live in hope of sharing in the everlasting life of God.[34]

The brave and submissive dispositions of Peter, Paul, Job, and Jesus have been exquisitely expressed in this testimony of an unknown Confederate soldier:

I asked God for strength, that I might achieve.
I was made weak, that I might learn humbly to obey.
I asked for health, that I might do greater things,

I was given infirmity, that I might do better things.
I asked for riches, that I might be happy,
I was given poverty, that I might be wise.
I asked for power, that I might have the praise of men.
I was given weakness, that I might feel the need of God.
I asked for all things, that I might enjoy life,
I was given life, that I might enjoy all things.
I got nothing that I asked for—but everything I had hoped for.
Almost despite myself, my unspoken prayers were answered.
I am, among all men, most richly blessed.

In his Romans letter Paul tells of a festering thorn that gave
him "unceasing anguish." He was distressed that only a few of
his fellow "Israelites" viewed Christianity as a continuation
and transformation of the ancient Hebrew religion.[35] In discussing his failings as a Christian witness to other Jews, the
apostle identified with an episode from Elijah's life. That despairing prophet was strengthened at Mount Sinai in a manner
he least expected. His fearful flight there followed a feisty fight
with the many prophets of Baal on Mount Carmel. At that
contest Elijah proved to the spectators' satisfaction that his
God and not Baal could miraculously ignite the wood beneath
a sacrificial animal. He retreated to Sinai with hopes of receiving reassurances from a divine epiphany like the one on Carmel that would stifle his doubts that Yahweh was more powerful than the storm god who was worshipped by his adversary,
Queen Jezebel. The prophet was listening for a revelation
which a psalmist claimed to have had:

Yahweh's voice kindles flashing fire;
Yahweh's voice causes upheaval in the wilderness....
Yahweh's voice twists the trees and strips the forests.[36]

At Sinai, however, Elijah did not hear God speaking
through extraordinary phenomena of nature as he had antici-

pated. Even though Israelite tradition had claimed that the Lord descended on Sinai in fire when he spoke to Moses,[37] Elijah's experience was different. The Elijah story states that the Lord was not in the hurricane, earthquake, or lightening, but in "a still small voice." The prophet learned that the revelation of God is best found in quiet changes in the social order rather than in the terrifying display of amoral omnipotence. He realized that many were still loyal to the Lord and that he should leave his wilderness retreat to appoint new political and religious leaders and to work with others who shared his convictions.[38]

Judging from the Pauline letters, the apostle was not at all interested in Elijah the miracle worker, even though that role was prominent in the scriptural account of the prophet, and it was what the Judaism of his day tended to focus upon when remembering him. Paul's only reference to Elijah tells of his learning, during a period of despondency, that God works in a quiet manner. When he was confronted with widespread Israelite religious unfaithfulness, that prophet thought that he was the only member of the God-squad. The apostle writes: "What does the divine voice say to him? 'I have kept for myself seven thousand persons who have not worshiped Baal.' So too at the present time there is a remnant left of those whom God had chosen by grace."[39] Paul may have found in that portion of the Elijah saga what some interpreters regard as a landmark developed in the Hebrew religion. The passage displays that a crucial discovery has been made—that God is not a fitful, coercive force but a persistent, persuasive agent. The story of Elijah at Sinai not only transcends the primitive tendency to think that the power and presence of God is best found in the apparent irregular convulsion of nature, but it also criticizes the self-righteous presumption that there is left only one's self doing the Lord's work. It graphically shows that God often does not work in the tempestuous ways that some religious leaders expect but is disclosed, in calm, non-sensational activities. When Paul felt dejected over what he considered to be a continual problem of Jewish unbelief—the rejection of Jesus as the promised Messiah—he was encouraged by the story of an inconspicuous but important remnant who shared Elijah's faith even though he had overlooked them.

"God moves in a mysterious way," but not, as hymn writer William Cowper would have it, by riding upon the storm in a Canaanite fertility god fashion. Phillip Brooks expressed Elijah's new understanding and transforms it in his Christmas carol:

> How silently, how silently, the wondrous gift is given!
> So God imparts to human hearts the blessing of his heaven.
> No ear may hear his coming, but in this world of sin,
> Where meek souls will receive him, still the dear Christ enters in.

Although Paul displays no interest in nativity stories of Jesus, with their accounts of supernatural angel visitations and a magical star, his doctrine was existentially concerned with the regeneration that occurs when the spirit of Christ becomes alive within a person in any time or place. Employing a maternal metaphor, Paul once wrote: "I am in labor until you take the shape of Christ."[40]

Habakkuk is another Israelite prophet who had an impact on Paul. Skeptical questions about divine justice were raised by Habakkuk, but he became convinced that, in spite of his inability to understand the way God was working internationally, he should be patient and trust that God's will was being fulfilled. In composing his theological essay for the Roman Christians, Paul borrowed from Habakkuk this main theme: "He who is righteous by faith shall live."[41] The best expression of faith in the Habakkuk prophecy is contained in this concluding affirmation:

Though the fig trees and the vines bear no fruit,
The olive crop fails and the fields produce no grain,
The sheep die and there are no cattle in the stalls,
I will still rejoice in the Lord and joy in the God of my
salvation.[42]

Characteristic of the Hebrew prophetic books, Habakkuk
does not extol supernaturalism. Faithfulness to God is in no
way based on the expectation that the Creator's works must
continually satisfy human wants. For Paul, as for Habakkuk,
religion was separated from the arrogant assumption that
nature's productivity must cater to localized human needs if
God is to be worshipped. Habakkuk and Paul did not think of
religion as a device for getting what one wants any more than
did the agonizing Jesus in the Garden of Gethsemane who
prayed: "Take this cup of suffering away from me. Yet not
what I will, but what you will."[43]

The piety of Jesus and Paul was like that of a psalmist, and
unlike that of a patriarch. Jacob vowed that he would serve
God if personal success were granted, but a psalmist expresses
confidence in God's presence "even though I walk through the
valley of the shadow of death."[44] Paul followed Jesus in maintaining that theological depth is measured by trust in God
when things do not turn out to be an individual's personal
advantage.

Suppose Paul had been asked to compose a brief creed that
would affirm the fundamental theology and practice of Christianity. What would he accept and what would he reject from
what is now found in the New Testament? He would not
mention a mythological conception by the Holy Spirit or
descent to an underworld after death. The *exclusive* sonship of
Jesus and the resurrection of the *flesh* would not be acceptable
phrases. In later life he probably would not have referred to

Jesus' return to this earthly realm after ascending to an overworld.

That apostle's creed might have declared the way in which the Ultimate became intimate in this Christocentric manner:

> I believe in the God of grace, wisdom, and power who is expressed in the continuing creation and in Christ Jesus.[45] Although he was the true image of God, he did not snatch at divine equality.[46] Jesus was born into a particular human community and grew up in obedience to the Jewish law.[47] He witnessed gently, loved sacrificially, suffered joyfully, and served humbly.[48] By being crucified for our sins he overcame our alienation from God and established a new covenant based on freedom and responsibility.[49] God has highly exalted Jesus as Lord and has resurrected all who are part of his forgiving and trusting fellowship.[50] By participating in the Lord's Supper I share in God's inclusive family, with Christ as elder brother, now and forever more.[51]

This look into the inner sanctum of Paul's religion gives grounds for rejecting theologian William Wrede's position that Paul was determined to "crush out the man Jesus" and replace him by "a superhuman...celestial being."[52] A number of influential scholars have endorsed that erroneous interpretation, including Wilhelm Bousset who held that Paul transformed the down-to-earth gospel of the "historical Jesus" into an otherworldly salvation scheme of the "supernatural Christ."[53]

This interpretation has been encouraged by a misunderstanding of a comment of Paul: "Though we once regarded Christ from a human point of view, we regard him thus no longer."[54] The apostle cannot have meant by this statement that he depreciated the historical Jesus for, as Josef Blank has shown, he relies on the tradition about Jesus in about two dozen places in his letters.[55] Paul was rather acknowledging that in his pre-Christian years he had wrongly rejected Jesus because of his shameful crucifixion which, from a cultural point of view, was inappropriate for God's Messiah.

The early church added a mythological layer that gave the Christ figure a supernaturalism similar to that which was prevalent among other ancient cult figures. E.R. Dodds has observed that in the opening centuries of Christianity "the human qualities and human sufferings of Jesus play singularly little part."[56] This is clear from the absence of the crucifixion motif in early Christian art. However, as we have demonstrated, Paul should not be held responsible for that docetic depreciation of Jesus' humanity.

In deed as well as in creed, Paul's religion was centered in the historical Jesus. In his life the rhythms of liberty and service, joy and compassion—that also pulsated through Jesus—were ended by his becoming the innocent victim of a violent death from the government. Those who wish to get back to Jesus must go through this apostle's life and thought for, as Hans Küng has also concluded, "Paul succeeded more clearly than anyone in expressing what is *the ultimately distinguishing feature* of Christianity:...*Jesus Christ crucified*."[57]

Paul separated, as all with high appreciation of the intellect should, the gospel from supernaturalism. He would probably have agreed with Küng's forthright judgment: "A supernatural intervention by God in the world would be nonsense. Physically, the consequences would be unthinkable if God were to suspend even for a moment the rules of that system which he himself laid down."[58] Were our religion based on a divine Puppeteer who accomplishes his will by jerking strings lowered to the earth, there could be no sciences. This is a high price that few moderns want to pay. Rudolf Bultmann, the most influential New Testament interpreter of our century, has encouraged Christians to "demythologize," that is, to discard the obsolete, supernatural world-view. His aim is not a negative one—to leave only scientific secularism to fill the void; rather, Bultmann uses Paul's language to express the hope that Christians "will eliminate a false stumbling-block and bring into sharp focus the real stumbling block, the word of the cross."[59] Since Paul, more than any other person who has ever lived, understood "the word of the cross" and thereby had the most competent grasp of the mind of Christ, we should use him as our guide for comprehending Christianity.

NOTES

Introduction

1. William Reese, *Dictionary of Philosophy and Religion* (Atlantic Highlands, N.J., 1980).

2. Cf. Andrew White, *A History of the Warfare of Science with Theology in Christendom* (New York, 1896), Vol. 2, pp. 5-15.

3. E.g., Martin Noth, *Exodus* (Philadelphia, 1962), p. 74; Walter Harrelson, *Interpreting the Old Testament* (New York, 1964), p. 82.

4. Cf. Robert Pfeiffer, *Religion in the Old Testament* (New York, 1961), p. 46.

5. Coert Rylaarsdam, "Exodus," *The Interpreter's Bible* (Nashville, 1952), Vol. 1, p. 838.

6. Artapanus, *Concerning the Jews* 23-32; quoted in Eusebius, *Praeparatio Evangelica* 9, 27. For Greek text and English translation see David L. Tiede, *The Charismatic Figure as Miracle Worker* (Missoula, 1972), pp. 317-324.

7. C. Milo Connick, *Jesus, the Man, the Mission, and the Message* (Englewood Cliffs, 1963), p. 281.

159

8   W.E. Phipps, *The Use of Jewish Scriptures by the Apostle Paul* (unpublished dissertation: University of St. Andrews, Scotland, 1954); *Encounter Through Questioning Paul: A Fresh Approach to the Apostle's Life and Letters* (University Press of America, 1983).

Chapter 1

The Thirst for Unnatural Happenings

1   Augustine, *Contra Faustus* 26, 3.
2   Augustine, *Confessions* 4, 4-6; 5, 6.
3   Augustine, *City of God* 3, 15.
4   Augustine, *Sermons on the Gospel of John* 8.
5   Paul Tillich, *Systematic Theology* (Chicago, 1951) Vol. 1, p. 116.
6   D.M. Brown, *Ultimate Concern: Tillich in Dialogue* (New York, 1965), p. 158.
7   C.S. Lewis *Miracles* (London, 1947), p. 15.
8   Brown, *op cit.*, pp. 159, 161.
9   Paul Tillich, *What is Religion?* (New York, 1969), pp. 107-108.
10   E.g., Isa. 21:4; 29;23; Jer. 44:12.
11   E.g., Job 5:9; Ps. 26:7; 40:5; 71:17; Isa. 29:14.
12   R.F. Johnson, "Signs and Wonders," *The Interpreter's Dictionary of the Bible* (Nashville, 1962).
13   Gal. 3:5;1 Cor. 12;10, 28-29; Rom. 15:18-19.
14   Rom. 15:19; 2 Cor. 12:12; 2 Thess. 2:19.
15   William Sanday, *et al. Miracles* (London, 1911), pp. 5-8. See also, Vernon McCasland, "Signs and Wonders," *Journal of Biblical Literature* 76 (1957), p. 151.
16   W.M. Ramsay, *The Bearing of Recent Discovery on the Trustworthiness of the New Testament* (London, 1915), p. 118.
17   Rom. 1:16.
18   1 Thess. 5:21.
19   Gal. 6:7.
20   Rom. 1:24-28; cf. C.H. Dodd, *The Epistle of Paul to the Romans* (London, 1932), p. 29.
21   Gerd Theissen, *The Miracle Stories of the Early Christian Tradition* (Philadelphia, 1983), p. 274.
22   Matt. 5:44; Luke 23:34; Acts 7:60.
23   1 Cor. 1:26-31.
24   Phil. 2:6-8.

25   1 Cor. 1:18.

26   Rom. 1:3; Gal. 4:4.

27   2 Cor. 8:9.

28   Phil. 2:6-7.

29   2 Cor. 10:1.

30   1 Cor. 7:10; Rom. 15:2-3.

31   Rom. 8:14-29.

32   1 Cor. 11:23-26.

33   2 Thess. 2:9.

34   Tertullian (*Contra Marcion* 3, 3), in contrast to Marcion, was later to reiterate that supernatural portents are, for the same reason, of no apologetic value.

35   Gal. 5:19-22.

36   2 Cor. 11:5, 22-23; 12:11.

37   2 Cor. 11:4; 12:12.

38   James M. Robinson and Helmut Koester, *Trajectories Through Early Christianity* (Philadelphia, 1971), p. 60.

39   Dieter Georgi, *Die Gegner des Paulus im 2 Korintherbrief* (Neukirchen, 1964), pp. 110-112.

40   Georgi, "Corinthians, Second Letter to the," *The Interpreter's Dictionary of Bible* (supplement) (Nashville, 1976).

41   John Gager, *Moses in Greco-Roman Paganism* (New York, 1972), p. 164.

42   2 Cor. 4:6.

43   2 Cor. 3:13-14.

44   Robinson and Koester, *op cit.*, p. 218.

45   Ernst and Marie-Luise Keller, *Miracles in Dispute* (Philadelphia, 1969), p. 190.

46   Cf. Mark 15:29-32.

47   Dennis Duling, *Jesus Christ Through History* (New York, 1979), p. 58.

48   Paul J. Achtemeier, "Pre-Marcan Miracle Catenae," *Journal of Biblical Literature* 89 (1970), pp. 265-291; "The Origin and Function of the Pre-Marcan Miracle Catenae," *Journal of Biblical Literature* 91 (1972), p. 198.

49   J. Christiaan Beker, *Paul the Apostle* (Philadelphia, 1980), p. 300.

50   Ex. 14:21-22.

51   2 Kings 2:8, 14.

52   *Baba Mezia* 59b; *Berakoth* 9, 1.

53   Mark 4:35-41.

54   1 Kings 21:20-24; 2 Kings 1:8; 2:6-9.

[55]   Mark 1:2-8; 6:16-18.

[56]   Cf. Louis Ginzberg, *The Legends of the Jews* (Philadelphia, 1910), Vol. 3, p. 239.

[57]   Mark 1:23-26; 1:29-31; 1:32-34; 1:40-45; 2:1-12; 3:1-6; 3:7-12; 4:35-41; 5:1-20; 5:25-34; 5:35-43; 6:32-44; 6:45-52; 6:53-56; 7:24-30; 7:31-37; cf. Wolfgang Roth, "The Secret of the Kingdom," *The Christian Century* 100 (1983), pp. 181-182.

[58]   2 Kings 4:42-44; Mark 6:30-44; 8:1-10.

[59]   2 Kings 5:10-14, Mark 1:40-45; 2 Kings 6:20, Mark 10:52.

[60]   1 Kings 17:21-23; 2 Kings 4:32-37.

[61]   Mark 5:35-43; 6:15.

[62]   Sirach 48:4-5; 48:10.

[63]   Rom. 11:2-3.

[64]   Cf. W. Grundmann, *"dynamai/dynamis,"* in *Theological Dictionary of the New Testament* (Grand Rapids, 1964).

[65]   Diogenes Laertius, *Lives of the Philosophers* 8, 59, and 67.

[66]   Justin, *Apology* 1, 22.

[67]   Mark 7:48.

[68]   Porphyry, *Life of Pythagoras* 29; cf. Iamblichos, *Life of Pythagoras* 135.

[69]   William N. Brown, *The Indian and Christian Miracles of Walking on the Water* (Chicago, 1928), p. 13.

[70]   Philostratus, *Apollonius of Tyana* 1, 5.

[71]   *Ibid.*, 3, 38-39; 4, 45; 8, 30.

[72]   Pliny, *Natural History* 7, 37, 124; Celsus, *On Medicine* 2, 6, 16.

[73]   Mark 5:22-43.

[74]   Tacitus, *History* 4, 81; Suetonius, *Vespasian* 7.

[75]   John Hull, *Hellenistic Magic and the Synoptic Tradition* (London, 1974), pp. 73-86, 142-143.

[76]   Mark 9:23.

[77]   2 Cor. 12:7-10.

[78]   Mark 11:12-24.

[79]   1 Cor. 13:2.

[80]   Isa. 42:3; 53:3-7; Phil. 2:5-8.

[81]   Theissen, *op. cit.*, p. 17.

[82]   Matt. 28:18.

[83]   Matt. 21:19.

[84]   Mark 5:22-23; Matt. 9:18.

[85]   Matt. 20:29-34; Mark 10:46-52.

[86]   Luke 4:26-27.

[87]   1 Kings 17:8-24.

[88]   Luke 7:11-16; 8:49-56; 9:10-12.

89 Luke 5:12-15; 17:11-19.
90 Luke 5:4-8; cp. Mark 1:16.
91 Mark 14:47; Luke 22:51.
92 Paul J. Achtemeier, "The Lucan Perspective on the Miracles of Jesus," *Journal of Biblical Literature* 94 (1975), p. 560.
93 Plutarch, *Romulus* 28.
94 Suetonius, *The Deified Augustus* 100.
95 Justin, 1 *Apology* 21.
96 2 Kings 2:1-18.
97 Acts 1:9-11; 2:2-34.
98 Acts 2:5-11; 1 Cor. 14.
99 Acts 2:22.
100 Marvin Miller, *The Character of Miracles in Luke-Acts* (microfilm: Ann Arbor, 1971), p. 126.
101 Acts 8:9-24.
102 Acts 9:32-41.
103 Acts 3:2-8; 14:8-10.
104 Acts 20:9-11.
105 Ernst Haenchen, *The Acts of the Apostles* (Philadelphia, 1971), p. 113.
106 Hisao Kayama, *The Image of Paul in the Book of Acts* (Ann Arbor, 1971), p. 154.
107 Ex. 7:8-13.
108 Acts 13:6-12.
109 Acts 16:16-18.
110 Acts 19:11.
111 Luke 10:19.
112 Acts 28:3-6.
113 *Tosefta Berakoth* 3, 20.
114 John 11:39.
115 John 2:1-11; cf. C.H. Dodd, *Historical Tradition in the Fourth Gospel* (Cambridge, 1965), pp. 224-225.
116 Pausanias, *Description of Greece* 6, 26, 2; Euripides, *The Bacchantes* 704-707.
117 Helmut Koester, *History and Literature of Early Christianity* (Philadelphia, 1982). p. 184.
118 Mark 3:15; Matt. 12:27; Luke 10:17.
119 John 9:32.
120 Theissen, *op. cit.*, p. 227.
121 Deut. 18:15; John 6:14.
122 Num. 16:28-31.
123 John 6:30.
124 John 6:14.

125 John 6:32-51.
126 2 Kings 2:9-22; John 1:19-2:11.
127 2 Kings 4:32-37; 5:1-14; John 4:46-54; 5:2-9.
128 2 Kings 4:42-44; John 6:1-14.
129 2 Kings 6:4-7; John 6:16-21.
130 2 Kings 13:20-21.
131 John 11:38-44.
132 Raymond Brown, "Jesus and Elisha," *Perspective* 12 (1971), pp. 85-89.
133 Sirach 48:13-14.
134 *Infancy Gospel of Thomas* 3; 4:1-5; 13:1-2.
135 E.A.W. Budge, *Legends of our Lady Mary* (Boston, 1922), pp. 71, 73, 75, 88, 91.
136 Acts 5:14-16.
137 *Acts of Peter* 21 and 13.
138 *Acts of Paul* 22-24.
139 *Acts of Peter* 27 and 28; *Acts of Paul* 2, 4, 8.
140 *Acts of Thomas* 33 and 81; *Acts of John* 23, 51-52, 75, and 80.
141 *Acts of Paul* 26 and 7.
142 *Acts of John* 60.
143 *Acts of John* 93.
144 Gregory of Nyssa, *Catechetical Oration* 34.
145 *Ibid.* 23.
146 Gregory the Great, *Dialogues* 1, 2; 2, 7.
147 *Ibid.* 1, 10; 2, 23.
148 *Ibid.* 4, 33.
149 Benedicta Ward, *Miracles and the Medieval Mind* (Philadelphia, 1982).
150 Keith Thomas, *Religion and the Decline of Magic* (New York, 1971), pp. 26, 31.
151 Alan Richardson, *Christian Apologetics* (London, 1947), p. 173.
152 Matthew Arnold, *Literature and Dogma* (Boston, 1874), p. 125.
153 Fyodor Dostoevsky, *The Brothers Karamazov* 1, 5, 5.
154 Morton Smith, *Jesus the Magician* (New York, 1978), p. 142.
155 Max Müller, ed., *Sacred Books of the East* (Oxford, 1879-1910), Vol. 47, p. 76.
156 *Dhammapada* 18, 254.
157 Cf. "Miracle," "Buddha," *Encyclopedia Britannica* (Chicago, 1974).
158 Koran 6, 110; 10, 21; 13, 30; 21, 5-6; 29, 49; "Miracles" in Thomas Hughes, *A Dictionary of Islam* (Lahore, 1964).
159 C.Y. Glock and R. Stark, *Religion and Society in Tension* (Chicago, 1965), p. 95.
160 Cicero, *On Divination* 2, 28.

[161] E.g., Plutarch, *Camillus* 6; *Coriolanus* 38; Polybius, *History* 16, 12; Herodotus, *History* 2, 55-57, 73, 156; 4, 94-96, 105.

[162] Justin, *Dialogue with Trypho* 69, 7.

[163] Origen, *Contra Celsus* 1, 6.

[164] *Ibid.* 1, 28.

[165] Julian, *Against the Galileans* 99, 191, 213.

[166] E.R. Dodds, *Pagan and Christian in an Age of Anxiety* (New York, 1965), p. 125.

[167] Gal. 5:22-23.

Chapter 2

From Sexual to Asexual Birth

[1] M.M. Dawson, ed., *The Basic Teachings of Confucius* (New York, 1942), p. 145.

[2] J.B. Pritchard, ed. *Ancient Near Eastern Texts* (Princeton, 1955), p. 370.

[3] Thomas Boslooper, *The Virgin Birth* (Philadelphia, 1962), p. 166.

[4] John Otwell, *And Sarah Laughed* (Philadelphia, 1977), p. 192.

[5] Gen. 29:31; 30:22.

[6] Ps. 139:13.

[7] Ex. 14:21; 15:8.

[8] E.g., Gen. 6:3; Job 27:3; Isa. 32:15; 44:3-4; Ps. 104:30.

[9] Job 33:4.

[10] Hosea 1:10; cf. Deut 14:1; Isa. 43:6.

[11] Gen. 4:1.

[12] *Kiddushin* 30b.

[13] I. Abrahams, "Marriage (Jewish)," *Encyclopedia of Religion and Ethics* (Edinburgh, 1905).

[14] *Genesis Rabbah* 8,9.

[15] G, F. Moore, *Judaism* (Cambridge, 1927), Vol. 1, p. 437; J. Abelson, *The Immanence of God in Rabbinical Literature* (London, 1912), p. 207.

[16] Aboth 3:2; cp. Matt. 18:20.

[17] *Sotah* 17a.

[18] Philo, *On the Decalog* 107; *The Special Laws* 2, 2, 225.

[19] Philo, *On Abraham* 254.

[20] Philo, *On the Change of Names* 131, 137.

[21] Philo, *On the Cherubim* 40-47.

[22] Gal. 4:4.

23 Job 14:1; Luke 7:28.
24 Rom. 1:3-4.
25 Gal. 4:5-6; Rom. 8:15, 19; Mark 14:36.
26 Gal. 4:22, 29.
27 John 1:18, 34, 45; 6:42.
28 John 1:12-13.
29 John 3:6-7.
30 Matt. 1:1-17; 13:55.
31 C.T. Davis, "Tradition and Redaction in Matthew 1:18-2:23," *Journal of Biblical Literature* 90 (1971), p. 421.
32 Irenaeus, *Against Heresies* 3, 11, 7; 5, 1, 3.
33 Justin, *Dialogue with Trypho* 49.
34 Luke 2:48-49.
35 Luke 4:22.
36 Matt. 23:9.
37 E.g., B.H. Streeter, *The Four Gospels* (London, 1936), p. 268; F.C. Grant, *An Introduction to New Testament Thought* (Nashville, 1950), p. 230; R. Bultmann, *The History of the Synoptic Tradition* (Oxford, 1968), pp. 291, 304.
38 Cf. A. Plummer, *St. Luke* (New York, 1922), pp. 30-31.
39 E.g., P. Winter, "The Proto-Source of Luke 1," *Novum Testamentum* (1956), pp. 184-185; J. Moffatt, *An Introduction to the Literature of the New Testament* (New York, 1918), p. 267.
40 Judg. 13:2-25.
41 Deut. 22:23-24; 2 Sam. 3:14; Philo, *On the Special Laws* 3, 12; E. Neufeld, *Ancient Hebrew Marriage Laws* (London, 1944), p. 144.
42 Tobit 7:14-9:6.
43 *Kethuboth* 1, 5; *Yebamoth* 4, 10.
44 *Niddah* 1, 4.
45 *Tosephta Niddah* 1, 6.
46 Ex. 21:10.
47 M. Cohn, "Marriage," *The Universal Jewish Encyclopedia* (New York, 1948).
48 1 Cor. 7:2-4; cf. W. Orr and J. Walther, *1 Corinthians* (New York, 1976), p. 208.
49 "Parthenos," *Theological Dictionary of the New Testament* (Grand Rapids, 1968).
50 Gen. 34:3; Joel 1:8.
51 Homer, *Iliad*, 2, 514; Sophocles, *Trachiniae*, 1219; Aristophanes, *Nubes*, 530; J.H. Moulton, *The Vocabulary of the Greek Testament* (London, 1930) H.J. Leon, *The Jews of Ancient Rome* (Philadelphia, 1960), pp. 130, 232.

52   J.M. Ford, "The Meaning of 'Virgin'," *New Testament Studies* 12 (1966), p. 298.

53   Ruth 3:9; Ezek. 16:8.

54   G.B. Caird, *The Gospel of St. Luke* (New York, 1963), p. 31.

55   Cf. W. Eichrodt, *Theology of the Old Testament* (Philadelphia, 1961), pp. 152, 223.

56   Acts 13:2; 15:28.

57   Ignatius, *Trallians* 9, 1.

58   Ignatius, *Ephesians* 18, 2.

59   Ignatius, *Ephesians* 19, 1; *Smyrnaeans* 1, 1.

60   Ignatius, *Smyrnaeans* 13, 1.

61   Aristides, *Apology for the Christians to the Roman Emperor* 15, 1.

62   Justin, *Dialogue with Trypho* 48, 54.

63   Justin, *Idem*; *Apology* 1, 33.

64   Justin, *Dialogue with Trypho* 67.

65   Justin, *Apology* 1, 21.

66   Cf. E.R. Goodenough, *The Theology of Justin Martyr* (Jena, 1923), pp. 181, 238.

67   Tertullian, *Apology* 21, 9-14.

68   Plutarch, *Life of Alexander* 2.

69   Tertullian, *On the Flesh of Christ* 20.

70   W.E. Phipps, *Was Jesus Married?* (New York, 1970), pp. 133-141.

71   Cf. A.J. Toynbee, *A Study of History* (London, 1939), Vol. 1 pp. 267-269.

72   Porphyry, *Life of Pythagoras* 2.

73   Diogenes Laertius, *Lives of the Philosophers* 3, 2.

74   Suetonius, *Lives of the Caesars* 2, 94.

75   Philostratus, *Apollonius of Tyana* 1, 4 and 6.

76   Euripides, *The Madness of Hercules* 798-800.

77   *Lalitavistara* 6; cf. A. Foucher, *A Life of Buddha According to the Ancient Texts* (Westport, CN, 1963), pp. 23-30.

78   Jerome, *Against Jovinian* 1, 42.

79   Iranaeus, *Proof of the Apostolic Preaching* 32; Cf. 1 Cor. 15:45.

80   Iranaeus, *Against Heresies* 3, 21, 10.

81   Pseudo-Justin, *On the Resurrection* 3.

82   T. Walker, *Is Not This the Son of Joseph?* (London, n.d.), pp. 33-34.

83   *Gospel of Philip* 6.

84   *Ibid.*, 82 and 91.

85   *Ibid.*, 17.

86   Athanasius, *The Incarnation of the Word of God* 8,5.

87   K. Barth, *Church Dogmatics* (Edinburgh, 1956), Vol. 1/2, pp. 192-194.

[88] Jerome, *Against Jovinian* 1, 20.

[89] Matt. 1:25.

[90] Tertullian, *On the Flesh of Christ* 23.

[91] Mark 6:3; Tertullian, *On Monogamy* 8; *On the Flesh of Christ* 7.

[92] *The Protevangelium of James* 9:2; 19-20.

[93] Jerome, *Against Helvidius* 8; Luke 2:7; 7:12; 8:42.

[94] Jerome, *Letters* 48, 21; Song of Songs 4:12.

[95] Jerome, *Against the Pelagians* 2, 4: John 20:19, 26.

[96] Ezek. 44:2; Augustine, *On the Annunciation of the Lord* 3.

[97] Aquinas, *Summa Theologica* 3, q. 28, 3.

[98] *Ibid.*, 3, q. 28, 2; Luke 2:23.

[99] *Ibid.*, 3 supplement, q. 83, 3.

[100] *Ibid.*, 3, q. 28, 1; cf. Aristotle, *On the Generation of Animals* 729a.

[101] Cf. W.E. Phipps, "The Heresiarch: Pelagius or Augustine?" *Anglican Theological Review* 62 (1980), pp. 127-132.

[102] Aeschylus, *Eumenides* 11. 661-663.

[103] Cf. M. Warner, *Alone of All Her Sex* (New York, 1976), pp. 236-238.

[104] Aquinas, *op cit.* Mary was not "sanctified before animation" (3, q. 27, 2) and was "wholly conceived in original sin" (3, q. 31, 7).

[105] H. Morris, *The Battle for Creation* (San Diego, 1976), p. 308.

[106] G.D. Kaufman, *Systematic Theology* (New York, 1968), p. 203.

[107] P. Tillich, *Theology of Culture* (New York, 1959), p. 66.

[108] D. Bonhoeffer, *Christ the Center* (New York, 1966), p. 104.

[109] Jerome, *Against Helvidius* 21.

[110] Origen, *Against Celsus* 1, 37.

[111] Cf. W.E. Phipps, *Recovering Biblical Sensuousness* (Philadelphia, 1975), pp. 48-66, 83-86.

[112] J.A.T. Robinson, "Our Image of Christ Must Change," *Christian Century* 90 (1973), p. 340.

[113] C. Darwin, *The Origin of Species*, (London, 1860) Chap. 15; *The Descent of Man* (London, 1871) Chap. 21; cf. W.E. Phipps, "Darwin and Cambridge Natural Theology," *Bios* 54 (1983), pp. 218-227.

[114] M. P. Strommen, *et al.*, *A Study of Generations* (Minneapolis, 1972), p. 380.

[115] George Gallup and David Poling, *The Search for America's Faith* (Nashville, 1980), pp. 137, 139.

[116] C.Y. Glock and R. Stark, *Religion and Society in Tension* (Chicago, 1965), p. 95.

[117] Strommen, *op. cit.*, p. 379.

Chapter 3

The Growth of a Materialized Resurrection

1. 1 Cor. 9:1-2; Gal. 1:1, 12.
2. Norman Perrin, *The Resurrection According to Matthew, Mark, and Luke* (Philadelphia, 1977), pp. 82-83.
3. Phil. 3:4-5; Gal. 1:4.
4. Berakoth 28b.
5. Josephus, *Antiquities* 17, 2, 4.
6. Phil. 3:6.
7. Deut. 21:23; Gal. 3:13.
8. Gal. 1:12-17.
9. Jer. 1:5.
10. Gal. 2:20.
11. Phil. 3:8-10.
12. Rom. 6:5-6.
13. 2 Cor. 13:5.
14. 2 Cor. 5:17.
15. Col. 3:1, 12-14.
16. 2 Cor. 4:6.
17. Ex. 3:2.
18. Deut. 4:1-12.
19. Isa. 6.
20. Emile Calliet, *Pascal* (New York, 1961), pp. 131-132.
21. Paul Tillich, *Systematic Theology* (Chicago, 1957), Vol. 2, pp. 156-157.
22. Plato, *Republic* 527e, 533d.
23. 1 Cor. 9:1.
24. Rudolf Otto, *The Idea of the Holy* (New York, 1958), pp. 224-225.
25. 1 Cor. 15:16, 20, 49; Phil. 3:21.
26. 1 Cor. 15:40-44, 50.
27. 1 Cor. 6:13.
28. 1 Cor. 15:20.
29. 2 Cor. 5:8.
30. Thomas Best, "St. Paul and the Decline of the Miraculous," *Encounter* 44 (1983), p. 236.
31. Willi Marxsen, *The Resurrection of Jesus of Nazareth* (Philadelphia, 1970), p. 69.
32. 1 Cor. 15:54.
33. Rom. 2:7.

34   Rom. 6:23.

35   Phil. 3:19.

36   R.H. Charles, *Eschatology* (London, 1913), p. 444.

37   John 5:28-29.

38   Luke 24:34.

39   1 Peter 3:18; 4:6.

40   1 Peter 1:4, 23.

41   1 Cor. 15:53.

42   Luke 24:4, 23.

43   Luke 24:9.

44   Luke 24:15, 31, 39-43.

45   Ps. 16:10; Acts 2:27, 31; 13:35.

46   Gal. 1:18-19.

47   James M. Robinson, "Jesus from Easter to Valentinus (or to the Apostles' Creed)," *Journal of Biblical Literature* 101 (1982), pp. 12-16.

48   2 Baruch 50:2-3.

49   Matt. 27: 52-53.

50   John 12:2; 21:13.

51   Arthur McGiffert, *A History of Christian Thought* (New York, 1932), Vol. 1, pp. 88-89, 142.

52   2 Clement 9:1.

53   Justin, *Dialogue with Trypho* 80.

54   Justin, *Apology* 1, 8.

55   Athenagoras, *On the Resurrection of the Dead* 8 and 25.

56   1 Cor. 15:50.

57   Irenaeus, *Against Heresies* 1, 30, 13; 5, 9, 1; 5, 11, 1; 5, 14, 4; 5, 7, 1; 5, 15, 1; 5, 12, 6; 5, 13, 1.

58   *The Gospel of Peter* 10.

59   Cf. Wilhelm Schneemelcher, ed., *New Testament Apocrypha* (Philadelphia, 1965), Vol. 1, p. 165.

60   *Epistula Apostolorum* 11; cf. *Ibid.*, p. 197.

61   Tertullian, *On the Veiling of Virgins* 1; *On Prescription Against Heresies* 13.

62   Tertullian, *On the Flesh of Christ* 5.

63   Luke 24:39.

64   Tertullian, *On the Resurrection of the Flesh* 48.

65   *Ibid.*, 63.

66   *Ibid.*, 50; 1 Cor. 15:50.

67   *Ibid.*, 57 and 60.

68   *Ibid.*, 32 and 42.

69   J.N.D. Kelly, *Early Christian Creeds* (London, 1960), p. 165.

70 E.g., *Constitution of the Holy Apostles* 7, 41; cf. John Leith, ed., *Creeds of the Churches* (New York, 1963), pp. 23-25.

71 Origen, *First Principles* 2, 10, 1-3.

72 Origen, *Against Celsus* 5, 14-24.

73 Jerome, *Letters* 108, 23; *To Pammachius Against John of Jerusalem* 23.

74 Jerome, *Letters* 108, 24; *To Pammachius* 31.

75 Augustine, *Retractions* 1, 17.

76 Augustine, *Enchiridion*, 91.

77 Augustine, *City of God* 22, 15; *Enchiridion* 85-86.

78 Augustine, *City of God*, 22, 19-20.

79 *Ibid.*, 22, 17.

80 *Ibid.*, 22, 8.

81 Gregory of Nazianzen, *Funeral Orations* 80.

82 Aquinas, *Summa Theologica* 3, supplement, q. 77, 3; q. 79, 1.

83 R. Lawler, *et al.*, *The Teaching of Christ: A Catholic Catechism for Adults* (Dublin, 1976), p. 544.

84 Martin Luther, *Small Catechism*, q. 165.

85 John Calvin, *Theological Treatises* (Philadelphia, 1954), p. 43.

86 John Calvin, *Institutes of the Christian Religion* 3, 25, 7 and 8.

87 *Codex iuris canonici* (Rome, 1918) 1203, 1240.

88 Cf. John Ferguson, *The Religions of the Roman Empire* (New York, 1970), pp. 136-137.

89 Cf. M.B. Walsh, "Cremation," *New Catholic Encyclopedia* (New York, 1967).

90 Paul VI, "Instructio: De cadaverum crematione," May 8, 1963.

91 Paul VI, " The Divine Truth," *Vital Speeches*, Aug. 1, 1968, p. 612.

92 Alma 11:43-44.

93 Jacob 3:11.

94 Joseph F. Smith, *Gospel Doctrine* (Salt Lake City, 1969), pp. 22-23.

95 Joseph Smith, *Doctrine and Covenants* (1835), 132:15-19, 63.

96 When the term "fundamentalism" was coined early in this century, belief in Jesus' physical resurrection was one of those fundamentals. Christian fundamentalists number in the multi-millions. There are probably even more Christians in churches that are not ultra-conservative who hold this position. Cf. M.P. Strommen, *et al.*, *A Study of Generations* (Minneapolis, 1972), p. 111.

97 John Updike, "Seven Stanzas at Easter," *The Christian Century*, 78 (1961), p. 236.

98 Cf. Leo Rosten, ed., *Religions of America* (New York, 1975), pp. 99, 103, 205.

[99]   Plato, *Republic* 514-518.

[100] 1 Cor. 2:9, 14.

Chapter 4

Astrology, Angelology, and Christology

[1]   Morris Jastrow, *The Religion of Babylonia and Assyria* (Boston, 1898), pp. 458-459; S.H. Hooke, *Babylonian and Assyrian Religion* (Norman, Okla., 1963), pp. 94-95.

[2]   A. Sachs, "Babylor an Horoscopes," *Journal of Cuneiform Studies*, Vol. 6.

[3]   Plato, *Epinomis* 987.

[4]   *Ibid.*, 982-985.

[5]   Plato, *Symposium* 202-203.

[6]   Plato, *Timaeus* 41-42.

[7]   Gilbert Murray, *Five Stages of Greek Religion* (New York, 1925), pp. 177-178.

[8]   Proclus, *On Timaeus* 285.

[9]   Helmut Koester, *History, Culture, and Religion of the Hellenistic Age* (Philadelphia, 1982), pp. 158, 376.

[10] John Ferguson, *The Religions of the Roman Empire* (Ithaca, 1970), p. 154.

[11] Seneca, *Consolation to Marcia* 16.

[12] Suetonius, *Lives of the Caesars* 2, 94, 12.

[13] Dio Cassius, *History* 57, 15, 7-9; Jack Linsay, *Origins of Astrology* (London, 1971), p. 293.

[14] Suetonius, *Lives of the Caesars* 8, 14-17.

[15] Lawrence Jerome, *Astrology Disproved* (Buffalo, 1977), p. 30.

[16] Tacitus, *The Annals* 6, 22.

[17] Ptolemy, *Tetrabiblos* 3, 12.

[18] Vettius Valens, *Anthologies* 5, 9, 2.

[19] Franz Cumont, *Astrology and Religion Among the Greeks and Romans* (New York, 1912), p. 121.

[20] Origen, *Against Celsus* 6, 22.

[21] Jerome, *Letters* 107, 2.

[22] Edwyn Bevan, *Hellenism and Christianity* (London, 1921), p. 77.

[23] Ernst Zinner, *The Stars Above Us* (London, 1957), p. 85.

[24] E.g., 2 Kings 17:16; 23:4-5; Jer. 8:1-2; Amos 5:26-27; Acts 7:42.

[25] 2 Kings 21:3; Deut. 4:19; 18:10; Isa. 47:13.

[26] *Book of Jubilees* 12:16-18.

27 *The Sibylline Books* 3:219-226.

28 Cf. T.H. Gaster, "Angel," *The Interpreter's Dictionary of the Bible* (Nashville, 1962).

29 *"Aggelos," Theological Dictionary of the New Testament* (Grand Rapids, 1964), p. 79.

30 Tobit 12:14-15.

31 1 Enoch 71:10.

32 Jubilees 2:2; cp. 1 Enoch 60:17, 82:13.

33 *Book of Hymns* 1.

34 *Manual of Discipline* 3.

35 Robert Grant, *Gnosticism and Early Christianity* (New York, 1959), pp. 38-48.

36 Philo, *On Dreams* 1, 22 and 142.

37 Philo, *On Flight* 69.

38 Gal. 4:4.

39 2 Cor. 11:14.

40 Sirach 21:27.

41 2 Cor. 12:7.

42 1 Thess. 4:15-16; 2 Thess. 1:7-8.

43 Acts 23:8.

44 Gal. 1:8; 1 Cor. 13:1-3.

45 1 Cor. 6:3.

46 Gal. 3:19; cf. Acts 7:53.

47 1 Cor. 8:5-6.

48 1 Cor. 15:24.

49 Rom. 8:38-39.

50 Albert Schweitzer, *The Kingdom of God and Primitive Christianity* (London, 1968), p. 157; cf. *The Mysticism of St. Paul* (London, 1953), pp. 65-74.

51 Gal. 4:3, 9-11; 5:1.

52 Col. 2:8, 18.

53 Col. 2:20-21.

54 *"Pleroma," Theological Dictionary of the New Testament.*

55 Col. 1:15-18; 2:8.

56 Col. 2:16.

57 2 Thess. 1:9-10; Col. 1:27.

58 Grant, *op. cit.*, p. 159.

59 Irenaeus, *Against Heresies* 1, 24.

60 Gen. 6:1-4.

61 1 Enoch 10:4-12, 12:4-6; 16:1.

62 Jude 6-9, 14-15; 1 Enoch 1:9.

63 Rev. 5:11; 7:1.

64   Rev. 12:7-10; 20:1-3; cp. Job 1.
65   Linsay, *op. cit.*, pp. 395-396.
66   Ignatius, *Trallians* 5:2.
67   Justin, *Apology* 1, 6; 2, 5.
68   Ambrose, *On Widows* 9.
69   Council of Laodicea, canon 35.
70   A.A. Bialas, "Angels," *New Catholic Encyclopedia* (New York, 1966).
71   Pseudo-Dionysius, *Celestial Hierarchy* 4.
72   Adolph Harnack, *History of Dogma* (New York, 1961), Vol. 3, p. 252.
73   Aquinas, *Summa Theologica* 1, q. 52, 3.
74   Dante, *Paradise* 28, 98-138.
75   J.P. Kenny, "Supernatural," *New Catholic Encyclopedia.*
76   John Calvin, *Institutes* 1, 14, 4; 1, 14, 12.
77   *Emerging Trends* (Princeton, 1979), Vol. 1, No. 3, p. 2.
78   J.A.T. Robinson, *But That I Can't Believe* (New York, 1967), p. 123.
79   Billy Graham, *Angels: God's Secret Agents* (New York, 1975), pp. 15, 164.
80   *Ibid.*, pp. 49, 55, 92.
81   Theodore Wedel, *The Medieval Attitude Toward Astrology* (New Haven, 1920), p. 77.
82   Aquinas, *Summa Theologica* 1, q. 115, 4.
83   Roger Bacon, *Major Works* 1, 266.
84   "Astrology," *The Catholic Encyclopedia* (New York, 1913).
85   P.T.H. Naylor, *Astrology: An Historical Examination* (London, 1967), p. 56-57; W.E. Phipps, "Heaven's Alarm to the World," *Natural History*, Aug. 1985, pp. 6-8.
86   Wedel, *op. cit.*, pp. 28-29.
87   Bartolommeo Platina, *Lives of the Popes* (1865), p. 385.
88   Bertrand Russell, *A History of Western Philosophy* (New York, 1945), p. 502.
89   Cf. Lawrence Jerome, *op. cit.*, pp. 45, 139.
90   *Ibid.*, pp 1, 3.
91   Will Durant, *The Story of Civilization: Our Oriental Heritage* (New York, 1935), p. 80.
92   *Emerging Trends*, Vol. 1, No. 3, p.2; George Gallup, *Religion in America* (Princeton, 1982), p. 6.
93   Mircea Eliade, *Occultism, Witchcraft, and Cultural Fashions* (Chicago, 1976), pp. 59-61.
94   Gal. 5:1.

Chapter 5

Superman and Jesus

[1] 1 Kings 17-18; 2 Kings 1-2.
[2] 2 Kings 4:32-37, 42-44; 5:1-14; 13:21.
[3] Cf. Louis Ginzberg, *The Legends of the Jews*, Vol. 3, p. 410.
[4] Cf. "Miracles" in Thomas Hughes, *A Dictionary of Islam*.
[5] I.K. Taimni, *The Science of Yoga* (Madras, 1961), p. 346, commenting on *Yoga Sutras* 3, 40; cf. *Rig Veda* 10, 136.
[6] Apollodorus, *Library* 2, 5.
[7] Gerd Theissen, *The Miracle Stories of the Early Christian Tradition*, p. 267.
[8] Lucian, *Philosophers for Sale* 2.
[9] Lucian, *The Passing of Peregrinus* 13; *The Liar* 13.
[10] *Acts of Peter* 32.
[11] *American Baptist Magazine*, Feb., 1979, p. 3; *Newsweek*, Jan. 1, 1979, p. 50; John 11:25.
[12] *The Gospel of Pseudo-Matthew* 22.
[13] Luke 2:52; 1 Sam. 2:26.
[14] Heb. 4:15.
[15] Cf. W.E. Phipps, *Was Jesus Married?*, pp. 34-70; 1 Cor. 7:25; 9:5.
[16] Matt. 4:5-7; Luke 4:9-12.
[17] James 5:16-18.
[18] Cf. Geza Vermes, *Jesus the Jew* (New York, 1973), pp. 69-79.
[19] *Taanith* 3, 8.
[20] *Taanith* 24b; *Yoma* 53b.
[21] Matt. 5:45; 7:24-27.
[22] Aristotle, *Physics* 198b, 17-23.
[23] Sigmund Freud, *New Introductory Lectures on Psychoanalysis* (New York, 1964), p. 146.
[24] Luke 11:29-32; Matt. 12:38-42.
[25] Mark 8:12.
[26] Matt. 12:40.
[27] Luke 16:19-31.
[28] Luke 11:19.
[29] Luke 5:12-6:26; Mark 6:5.
[30] Luke 4:40-44.
[31] Isa. 42:1-4; 49:6; cf. W.E. Phipps, "Jesus, the Prophetic Pharisee," *Journal of Ecumenical Studies* 14 (1977), p. 25.
[32] Mark 15:29-39.

33   Rom. 8:39; 5:8.
34   *Luthers Werke* (Weimar, 1883-), Vol. 7, p. 586.
35   Ian Siggins, *Martin Luther's Doctrine of Christ* (New Haven, 1970), p. 42.
36   Shusaku Endo, *A Life of Jesus* (New York, 1978), p. 173.
37   1 Peter 2:21.
38   Frederic Myers, "Saint Paul," in *Poems* (London, 1870), p. 13.

Conclusion

1   1 Cor. 15:9.
2   2 Cor. 12:2.
3   Rom. 2:16; 16:25.
4   2 Cor. 8:13-15.
5   Rom. 14:14; 1 Cor 6:19; 10:25-26.
6   Cf. W.E. Phipps, "Is Paul's Attitude toward Sexual Relations Contained in 1 Cor. 7:1?" *New Testament Studies* 28 (1982), pp. 125-131.
7   2 Cor. 4:7-12.
8   Col. 2:9-10; 3:12-14.
9   Cf. 2 Peter 3:15-16.
10   Albert Schweitzer, *The Mysticism of Paul the Apostle*, (New York, 1960), p. 377.
11   1 Cor. 14:15.
12   Gerd Theissen, *The Miracle Stories of the Early Christian Tradition*, (Philadelphia, 1983) p. 246.
13   Spinoza, *Tractatus Theologico-Politicus* (1670) 11; 1 Cor. 10:15.
14   1 Cor. 14:19-20.
15   Frederick Ferré, "Ecstasy and Intelligence," *The Christian Century* 98 (1981), p. 1059.
16   2 Cor. 5:19.
17   Tertullian, *On Prescription Against Heretics* 7.
18   *Time*, Nov. 12, 1984, p. 112.
19   1 Cor. 3:1-2.
20   Rom. 1:20.
21   Francis Bacon, *Essays*, "Of Atheism."
22   Quoted in *The Boston Globe*, Nov. 9, 1984, p. 2.
23   1 Cor. 8:1-2.
24   Rom. 11:33.
25   Blaise Pascal, *Pensées* 253, 265.
26   1 Thess. 5:21; 2 Thess. 2:2-3.
27   Abelard, *Yes and No*, Preface.

28 1 Cor. 7:10-11, 11:23-25.
29 C.E. Raven, *The Earth is the Lord's* (London, 1954).
30 2 Cor. 4:7-9, 11.
31 2 Cor. 12:9.
32 Heb. 5:7-8.
33 1 Peter 1:19; 2:21-24; 4:11.
34 1 Peter 4:6, 8, 13.
35 Rom. 9:1-5.
36 Ps. 29:7-9.
37 Ex. 19:18.
38 1 Kings 19.
39 Rom. 11:4-5.
40 Gal. 4:19.
41 Hab. 2:4; Rom. 1:17.
42 Hab. 3:17-18.
43 Mark 14:36.
44 Gen. 28:20-21; Ps. 23:4.
45 2 Cor. 4:6; 5:17-19; Rom. 3:24; 8:19-23; 1 Cor. 1:24.
46 Col. 1:15; Phil. 2:6.
47 Gal. 4:4.
48 2 Cor. 10:1; Gal. 2:20; 1 Thess. 1:6; Phil. 2:7-8.
49 Col. 2:13-14; 2 Cor. 5:18; 1 Cor. 11:25; Gal. 5:1; 6:2.
50 Phil. 2:9-11; Rom 6:5; Col. 3:13; 1 Cor. 4:2.
51 1 Cor. 11:17-26; Rom 6:23; 8:21-29; 9:24.
52 William Wrede, *Paul* (Boston, 1908), pp. 87, 182.
53 Wilhelm Bousset, *Kyrios Christos* (Göttingen, 1921), p. 105; cf. H.J. Schoeps, *Paul* (Philadelphia, 1961), p. 58.
54 2 Cor. 5:16.
55 Josef Blank, *Paulus und Jesus* (Munich, 1968), pp. 129, 323-324.
56 E.R. Dodds, *Pagan and Christian in an Age of Anxiety*, (New York, 1965) p. 119.
57 Hans Küng, *On Being a Christian* (New York, 1976), pp. 409-410; 1 Cor. 2:2.
58 Hans Küng, *Does God Exist?* (New York, 1980), p. 653.
59 Rudolf Bultmann, *Jesus and Mythology* (New York, 1958), p. 36; cf. 1 Cor. 1:23.

INDEX